CYCLE TOURING IRELAND

Cycle Touring Ireland

Brendan Walsh

GILL & MACMILLAN

Gill & Macmillan Ltd
Goldenbridge
Dublin 8
with associated companies throughout the world
© text, Brendan Walsh 1992, 1997
© maps, Gill & Macmillan 1992, 1997
0 7171 2445 2
Maps by Justin May
Original text design by O'K Design, Dublin
Print origination by Carole Lynch
Printed by The Guernsey Press

This book is typeset in 8/10 pt Palatino.

A catalogue record for this book is available from the British Library.

1 3 5 4 2

Maps reproduced in this book are based on the Ordnance Survey by
permission of the Government (Permit No. 5574).

Contents

Foreword

Each year, I am privileged as a broadcaster and journalist on sports, mostly cycling, to fly around 150,000 miles and visit all of those exotic countries most of us dream of: Australia, America, South and East Africa, Hawaii. It is a bonus in my life of which I am acutely aware.

But I wonder how many of you who might be browsing through — or even buying — this marvellous guide realise that perhaps the nicest land of all is, to most of us, just a short journey away.

Politically, Ireland still has her difficulties but one thing the politicians can never take away is the beauty of Ireland as a whole — North and South — which, even as the year 2000 approaches, remains for many one of the greatest undiscovered corners of the world.

The blue waters of the Pacific Ocean on Hawaii, the sun-scorched Lowveld of Africa and even the tree-shrouded pavement of the Blue Ridge Parkway, all 250 miles of it, in the United States — none attracts me more than the lush, green hills and craggy sea inlets of an island with everything.

I admit it. I'm a cyclist of no repute and a holder of the scroll of the typically fine and historic town of Carrick-on-Suir. I discovered these lands and people many years ago and have returned ever since. I will never tire of the Ring of Kerry, the Mountains of Mourne, the Comeraghs, the Ards Peninsula or the big cities of Belfast, Dublin, Limerick and Cork.

Brendan Walsh, in updating his former *Irish Cycling Guide*, has produced *Cycle Touring Ireland*, with all the thoroughness needed for you to have many memorable visits. He has opened up yet more byways into pastures unknown even by me; more avenues of discovery where the people are guaranteed to offer that warm welcome and helpful advice typical of Ireland.

The bicycle, even if you have never ridden one, should not be feared. In Ireland, both North and South, the traffic-free roads are still meant for cycling. In this land of time enough, there is enough time, so take it all and enjoy a country that has defied the passage of time and remains one of the nicest places in the world to visit.

Especially by bike!

Phil Liggett
Hertfordshire
England
1997

Preface to the 1997 Edition

When I set out to write this Preface to the second edition of *Irish Cycling Guide* — now *Cycle Touring Ireland* — I realised that although the routes chosen for the 1992 edition had stood the test of time and have been generally applauded, a huge amount of other material had radically altered. Telex is obsolete, fax is king and more than half of the 1992 phone numbers had changed. In 1992 there were only six officially recognised privately owned hostels in the Republic of Ireland — now there are 132. Northern Ireland is still a long way behind: Dublin has nearly a dozen hostels as opposed to Belfast's (only) one. Apart from a few small corrections and the noting of relevant hostels in the text of the routes described, I have added some side attractions and advice, pubs and restaurants (marked ✓ at the bottom of the page) but only those I have personal knowledge of.

My thanks for advice and corrections (to the 1992 edition) to Philip Boulding, Vivian Matthews, the Grinder Dunleavy and Nordie Barry for Donegal researches, my brothers Rory, David and Johnny (all cyclists), Ruadhan MacEoin, Lynn and Scott Grannan and Martin Tillin, also Martine Kerr, Michael Roche and Patricia Harney for gastronomic advice. Particularly I would like to thank (the great photographer) Robert Vance for his patience and perception, Ray Shanks for his marketing advice, my patient secretary, Margaret Rubotham, both Michael Gill and Don Roberts (both keen cyclists) for their wider book-marketing skills, and my wife, Ruth, and our children, Sinead, Cara, Aifric and Oisin. Apart from that my renewed thanks is due to all those mentioned in the first edition, with special thanks to my cycling friends who believe (wrongly!) that they have prevented me from becoming too pompous.

This book — for what it is worth — remains dedicated to my mother Constance (Connie) Walsh.

Brendan Walsh
Dublin
January 1997

Preface to the 1992 Edition

Ireland has more miles of serviced roads per head of population than any country in Europe, and possibly the world! This, combined with its fairly temperate climate and stunning scenery, puts it in the top bracket for cycle tourists.

This book aims to bring cycle tourists to the most beautiful parts of Ireland as quickly as possible and on roads with the least traffic.

Taking the island of Ireland as a whole, from the east coast with its rolling hills through the midlands with its lakes, old towns, castles and churches to the west with its highlands, islands and fantastic coastline, the entire island has much to offer the cycle tourist, particularly in the way of traffic-free roads. Even the capricious weather has its own delight: a wet morning can be a fair guarantee of a fine afternoon!

In the course of writing this book, I have run up many debts of gratitude. I am grateful for the help and assistance given by Helen Kehoe and Noel Kavanagh of Bord Failte who were always available with statistics, figures, etc.; by Anne Moore of Northern Ireland Tourist Board for similar help; by Frank Lanigan for his West Cork advices (and for not seizing the book); John Murray for his words of wisdom; ('the') Shay O'Hanlon; Pat O'Callaghan and Josephine Glennon of the Federation of Irish Cyclists for their support; also by Frank Skelly for the original suggestion, Justin May for his very readable maps and Robert Vance for his photography; by my wife, Ruth, and children, Sinead, Cara, Aifric and Oisin, who had to show great perseverance; and my secretary, Margaret Rubotham, whose patience was sorely tried and tested.

This book is dedicated to my mother, Constance (Connie) Walsh, whom we would all like to have lived to see the day.

Brendan Walsh
Dublin
March 1992

Glossary

ITB	Irish Tourist Board, otherwise Bord Failte: the official tourist organisation for the Republic of Ireland.
NITB	Northern Ireland Tourist Board: the official tourist organisation for Northern Ireland.
IYHA	Irish Youth Hostel Association, otherwise An Oige: operates youth hostels in the Republic of Ireland.
YHANI	Youth Hostels Association of Northern Ireland: operates youth hostels in Northern Ireland.
IH	Independent Hostels Organisation: an association representing a large and expanding number of hostels operating mainly in the Republic of Ireland but with some hostels in Northern Ireland.
Iarnrod Eireann	Republic of Ireland (state-owned) national train service.
Northern Ireland Railways	Northern Ireland (state-owned) national train service.
Bus Eireann	Republic of Ireland (state-owned) national bus service.
Ulster Bus	Northern Ireland (state-owned) national bus service.
Aer Lingus	Republic of Ireland (state-owned) airline service.
OS	Ordnance Survey.
B & B	Bed and Breakfast.
Pub	Public house or non-residential inn.
Craic	Pronounced 'Crack' — there is no direct translation for this Irish phenomenon which is a mixture of fun, enjoyment, ambience and laughter.
Ceol	Irish for music.

Introduction

This book is geared to those cycle tourists who would do approx. 40 miles/64 km per day, bringing with them their own or hiring bicycles and either camping or staying in provided accommodation, whether youth hostel or hotel, bed & breakfast or guest house.

ACCOMMODATION
Hostels

In the Republic of Ireland the Irish Youth Hostel Association (IYHA) — otherwise An Oige — was founded in 1931, at the end of which year it had 215 members and two hostels. It now has 42 hostels located countrywide to provide good accommodation for those who like to travel or who like outdoor activities. Its hostels vary in size and type of building from a large mansion on 70 acres of lawns and woodlands (Aghadoe House, Killarney, Co. Kerry), a converted Norman castle (Foulksrath Castle, Co. Kilkenny), old coastguard stations and cottages to very modern buildings. Its headquarters is at 61 Mountjoy Street, Dublin 7, which is also one of its largest hostels. IYHA organises package holidays including cycling holidays. The organisation can be contacted at Dublin, Phone (01) 830 4555, Fax (01) 830 5808.

Youth Hostels Association of Northern Ireland (YHANI) was founded in 1931. YHANI is IYHA's sister organisation in Northern Ireland with eight youth hostels throughout Northern Ireland including Belfast. The Association can be contacted at Belfast, Phone (01232) 324733, Fax (01232) 439699.

When the first edition of this book, entitled *Irish Cycling Guide*, was published in 1992, there were then 18 privately owned hostels recognised by the Irish Tourist Board in the Republic of Ireland and none — so far as the author can establish — in Northern Ireland. They were styled Budget Hostels with their own association. Since then the number of hostels has increased considerably. The organisation which now represents them is the Independent Holiday Hostels Ireland (IHH) referred to in this book as IH. As at October 1996 there were 137 throughout both parts of Ireland, five of these in Northern Ireland and 132 in the Republic. The association can be contacted at Dublin, Phone (01) 836 4700, Fax (01) 836 4710, E-Mail IHH@Internet-Eireann.ie.

If planning a cycling tour of any part of Ireland, these organisations are anxious to facilitate you and can be contacted as above. The author recommends that cycle tourists should use hostels not only for economic reasons but because of their superb locations and because other cycle tourists will be met there.

All three organisations produce excellent guides to their hostels.

Camping
There are many campsites which are officially approved by ITB and NITB, though in most areas visited by this book there is no need to worry unduly about camping. Rough camping is where you find it, subject to the usual strictures against litter, etc., though the consent of the landowner should be obtained if camping in an enclosed field. Camping in public parks in towns and cities is inadvisable and is usually prohibited, particularly in Dublin's Phoenix Park. Note also that Dublin has no official campsite.

Bed & Breakfast/Hotels
B & Bs or hotels are not marked on any of the maps or listed in this book because B & Bs are everywhere to be found and, like hotels, are listed by ITB and NITB in excellent guides which can be obtained at any tourist office or by writing to the Irish Tourist Board at P.O. Box 273, Dublin 8 (for the Republic) or the Northern Ireland Tourist Board at 59 North Street, Belfast BT1 1NB (for Northern Ireland). See the Useful Telephone Numbers section, page 132.

BORD FAILTE/IRISH TOURIST BOARD
ITB — Bord Failte/Irish Tourist Board maintains offices throughout the Republic of Ireland as well as Northern Ireland and Great Britain, Europe, USA, Canada and Australia. It is charged with responsibility for the Irish tourist industry and brings out several excellent and very helpful booklets. Of interest to touring cyclists would be the following:
Approved Guest Accommodation, Dining in Ireland, Caravan & Camping Parks, Farm Holidays, County Guides, Hotels & Guest Houses.
In addition, Bord Failte produces publications on every conceivable tourist-related activity. It can be contacted at P.O. Box 273, Dublin 8, or Phone (01) 602 4000, Fax (01) 676 4764.

NORTHERN IRELAND TOURIST BOARD
NITB — Northern Ireland Tourist Board is charged with responsibility for the Northern Ireland tourist industry. It maintains offices in Dublin, London and Glasgow, France, Germany, USA, Canada and Australia. It produces booklets and information leaflets on accommodation, transport and tourist-related activities and can be contacted at St Anne's Court, 59 North Street, Belfast BT1 1NB, Phone (01212) 231221, Fax (01212) 240960.

Accommodation in Dublin City

Depending on the time of year, accommodation can be difficult to obtain in Dublin city. There are many hotels, guest houses, B & Bs and hostels but during the tourist season it is as well to pre-book.

Hostels that are open all year round include the following:

1. An Oige (Irish Youth Hostels Association), 61 Mountjoy Street, Dublin 7, Phone (01) 830 4555, Fax (01) 830 1600. (Also the headquarters of IYHA.)
2. Abraham House, 82–83 Lower Gardiner Street, Dublin 1, Phone (01) 855 0600, Fax (01) 855 0598.
3. Avalon House, 55 Aungier Street, Dublin 2, Phone (01) 475 0001, Fax (01) 475 0303.
4. Globetrotters Tourist Hostel, 46–48 Lower Gardiner Street, Dublin 1, Phone (01) 873 5893 and 874 0592, Fax (01) 878 8787.
5. 'Goin' My Way', 15 Talbot Street, Dublin 1, Phone (01) 878 8484 and 878 8091, Fax (01) 878 8091.
6. Isaac's Dublin, Frenchman's Lane (beside Central Bus Station), Dublin 1, Phone (01) 874 9321, Fax (01) 874 1574.
7. Kinlay House Christchurch, 2–12 Lord Edward Street, Dublin 2, Phone (01) 679 6644, Fax (01) 679 7437.
8. Marlborough Hostel, 81–82 Marlborough Street, Dublin 1, Phone (01) 874 7629 and 874 7812, Fax (01) 874 5172.

For those not wishing to avail of hostel accommodation, complete details of hostels, guest houses, B & Bs, etc., can be obtained from Dublin Tourism, Phone (01) 605 7777, Fax (01) 605 7787.

For those arriving in Dublin city who require reasonably priced and safe accommodation above hostel standard, the author specially recommends Clifden House, 32 Gardiner Place, Dublin 1, Phone (01) 874 6364, Fax (01) 874 6122. Clifden House is a family owned and operated guest house run by Jack and Mary Lalor, both of whom are keen cyclists. Jack in particular is an accomplished mountaineer and sub-aqua diver as well as being a keen cycle tourist and will be in a position to give advice on routes, methods of travel, where to stay and what to visit.

For those arriving on the south side of the city, particularly the Dun Laoghaire area, the author specially recommends John and Cathy O'Connor's B & B at 10 Corrig Avenue, Dun Laoghaire, which is only a few minutes from the ferry port — Phone and Fax (01) 280 0997. John and Cathy are accomplished cavers, sub-aqua divers and mountaineers as well as being enthusiastic cycle tourists, and will be in a position to give advice about routes, where to stay, what to see and where to go.

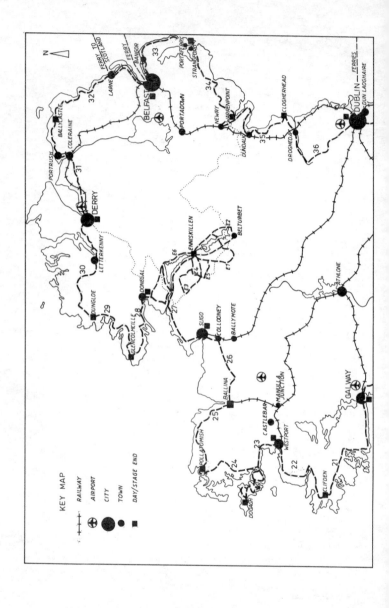

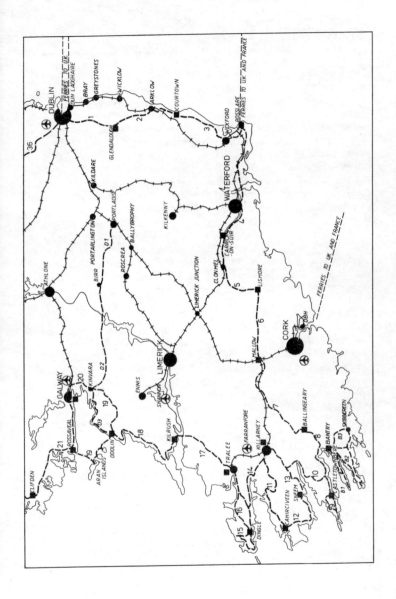

Travel to and in Ireland

From any entry point to Ireland either by land or sea you can easily link up with the routes suggested in this book. The book is geared to those tourists — whether from Ireland or overseas — who have limited time to spare, and for that reason it largely avoids the central area of Ireland. Accordingly, if your budget allows, you are advised to use trains to get to your chosen part of Ireland for cycle touring as quickly as possible. You should consider taking a train to the west coast of Ireland because the best cycle touring undoubtedly is on the western seaboard: West Cork, Kerry, Clare, Galway and Mayo. It is possible, for example, to leave Rosslare (1996 timetable and prices) at 07.15 and be in Killarney at 12.28 at a cost for one adult plus bicycle of approx. £41 return. Alternatively, using the same train and getting off at, say, Carrick-on-Suir cuts out the (pleasant but — by comparison with the west coast — drab) journey from Rosslare as far as Carrick-on-Suir after which, going west, there is some superb cycling. Leaving Rosslare at 07.15 and arriving at Carrick-on-Suir at 08.51 or Clonmel at 09.12 (cost for one adult with bike, single, £14 and £19 respectively) ensures that a full day's cycling can be had.

Trains

Bicycles can be taken on all Irish trains except for a few peak-hour trains and the DART (Dublin Area Rapid Transit) for a reasonable charge. They are carried in the guard's van at one end of the train. (Check with the station master before the train arrives which end the guard's van is situated, to avoid a rush down a crowded platform.) Carry elastic hooks to tie the bicycle upright to something. If intending to use trains a lot it would be advisable to check out special offers available from Iarnrod Eireann Travel Centres at 35 Lower Abbey Street, Dublin 1 or 65 Patrick Street, Cork or Phone Dublin (01) 836 6222. Northern Ireland Railways also take bikes at a very moderate charge.

Buses

There is a comprehensive network of Bus Eireann buses throughout Ireland, and Supabus coach services to Britain with connections to Europe. Full details can be obtained at Busaras, Store Street, Dublin 1, Phone (01) 836 6111 (for the Republic); and Ulsterbus at Milewater Road, Belfast BT3 9BS, Phone (01232) 351201 (for Northern Ireland). Buses will take bikes if there is room in the luggage area, which is not always the case unless the bus is a 'highliner' which usually would have room. It would be advisable if intending to travel with bicycle by bus that you present yourself in good time at the bus station. It would also be advisable to remove the pedals, turn the handlebars, etc., to make the bike more compact. There are many private bus companies operating in Ireland, details of which can only be obtained locally. They usually operate to and from Dublin, stopping at points in between.

Package Tours and Cycle Hire

Among those package tours available to cycle tourists are as follows:

1. IYHA offers cycling/hostelling holidays starting from Dublin (or other centres by arrangement) of one-, two-, three- and four-week duration. Prices depend on whether under or over 16 years of age and length of holiday. They include hire of bicycle, youth hostel overnight accommodation vouchers, youth hostel handbook and map. They are cycle-as-you-please and should be booked in advance. Enquiries to IYHA, 61 Mountjoy Street, Dublin 7, Phone (01) 830 4555, Fax (01) 830 5808.
2. Rent-a-Bike operates a package which includes bicycle and vouchers for use with farmhouses and guest houses. Prices vary depending on length of stay. Details from Rent-a-Bike, Phone (01) 872 5399, Fax (01) 836 4763.
3. Raleigh, the bicycle manufacturers, operate a Rent-a-Bike scheme from a large number of centres. They can be contacted c/o Hardings Bike Shop, 30 Bachelors Walk, Dublin 1, Phone (01) 873 2455, Fax (01) 873 3622.

In addition there are a number of specialist operators, details of which can be obtained from individual local TIOs throughout Ireland (see pp. 132–5) or the Federation of Irish Cyclists, North Circular Road, Dublin 7, Phone (01) 855 1522, Fax (01) 855 1771.

Bike Shops

Hardings Bicycle Shop, 30 Bachelors Walk, Dublin 1, which is 50 yards from O'Connell Bridge at the bottom of O'Connell Street in the centre of Dublin, has a good bike repair section and the shop carries a comprehensive range of bikes and cycling clothing, equipment and accessories. In addition they act as Central Booking Agency for Raleigh Rent-a-Bike (see section under Package Tours and Cycle Hire), Phone (01) 873 2455, Fax (01) 873 3622.

On the south side Martin O'Brien trading as Ringsend Cycles at 9 Bridge Street, Ringsend runs a small reliable bike repair shop with a small range of accessories, Phone (01) 668 4823.

In the Dún Laoghaire area The Bike Rack at 9 The Hill Centre, Johnstown Road, Dún Laoghaire is a reliable bike repair shop with a wide range of accessories, Phone (and Fax) (01) 284 0609.

Away from Dublin it is best to consult the Yellow Pages and best to phone in advance if possible as many of those listed would not carry a great range of spares.

Rules and Road Markings

Traffic in Ireland both North and South drives on the left. Until recently, road signs on roads in the Republic of Ireland were lettered and numbered as follows: T (for trunk) followed by a number e.g. T68, or (for less important roads) L (for link) followed by a number e.g. L23.

In each case the lettering/numbering was followed by a mileage. In recent years a complete re-lettering/re-numbering has commenced and will not be complete for some years to come. The new lettering/numbering is as follows: N (for national) followed by a number e.g. N38, or (for less important roads) R (for regional) followed by a number e.g. R24.

The old T roughly equates to the new N and the old L roughly equates to the new R — but only roughly! Any similarity between the two is purely in the letters, the numbers having no similarity whatsoever. This book tries to follow the designations in Michelin map 405.

N roads are usually well signposted so where they are used in this book T or L are not usually used. Sometimes only R (for Regional) designations are used; this is usually where the particular road has not been given a T or L designation but this situation is rare.

However, if seeking directions please bear in mind that Irish people are blissfully unaware of road designations and describe roads only by where they are headed, e.g. 'from Carrick-on-Suir take the road on the south side of the river 13 or 14 miles to Clonmel'.

Because most secondary roads still have signposts in miles this book mainly uses miles not kilometres. For quick conversion, 5 miles equals 8 kilometres almost exactly. Similarly, heights, where given, are in feet not metres. For quick conversion, 100 feet equals 30.5 metres.

Ireland has the greatest number of miles of serviced road of any country in Europe per head of population. In an effort to cut down on accidents at crossroads, many crossroads were altered so that the two lesser roads do not meet face on.

What used to be

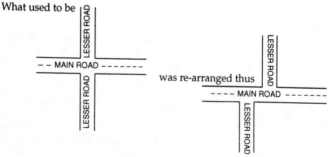

However, on all but the largest-scale maps these junctions will appear

If you come to what is a crossroads on the map but there is no facing road, then check left or right for 50 yards and your continuation road should be visible.

Signposts are not always accurate. They often get turned around accidentally, so if a signpost seems to be clearly wrong then check locally before proceeding; if needs be, flag down a car and ask directions.

Sometimes you will come across a junction with no signpost, in which case you can usually safely assume that if there are any white lines in the middle of the road these follow the main or more important road.

In the Republic, signposts are often in English and Irish. Sometimes, however, only the Irish is used so it is important to note:

Tra = strand or beach
Iascaigh = fishing
Geill Sli = give way
Banc = bank
Leitreas = toilets
Gardai = police
Oifig an Phoist = post office
Telefon = telephone

In Northern Ireland, the better roads are designated either by A followed by a number, or B followed by a number, e.g. A4 or B17. No effort has yet been made to use kilometres so that all signs are in miles. Although Northern Ireland roads have better road surfaces, they usually don't have hard shoulders as they do in the South, thus making them less enjoyable for cyclists.

Maps

There are many maps to assist the tourist in Ireland. By far the best for the cycle tourist is the Michelin sheet 405 at the scale of 1:400,000 (approx. 1 inch:6.3 miles) which covers the entire of the island of Ireland. Because this map, which covers the entire country, is clearly superior to all others on sale for cycle-touring purposes, most of the maps in this book have been drawn on the same scale so as to facilitate the combined use of this book with that map.

In the Republic of Ireland the Ordnance Survey half-inch series is very useful. They are indispensable if staying more than a day or two in any area or if you have a specific interest in a locality, its topography, geology, history, etc. The Ordnance Survey has also a number of maps of the more popular tourist areas on the scale of 1:50,000 and 1:25,000 and is planning more.

The Northern Ireland Ordnance Survey has an excellent series of maps on the scale of 1:50,000. In addition, there are privately published maps of certain areas. Of particular note and to be recommended are three maps, Oileain Arann (Aran Islands), The Burren and Connemara, all by Tim Robinson who has been highly commended by the British Cartographical Society for these works. They are essential to the enjoyment of these areas, and the entire set as a project won the Ford European Conservation Award for Ireland in 1987.

Weather

In Ireland winters are mild and the summers are temperate. July or, in some places, August is warmest, with temperatures averaging 58–59°F/14–15°C. February is coldest, when temperatures drop to 40–41°F/4–6°C. May and June are sunniest but not by much. Rain is heavier on the west coast than in the east and, naturally, heavier in the mountains. Snow is rare and, except in the mountains, doesn't last for long.

Phones and Codes

For phoning to the Republic of Ireland from outside the Republic of Ireland the prefix is 353, then add 1 (for Dublin) or, say, 61 for Limerick, followed by the particular number. For Northern Ireland, the international prefix is 08 (from the Republic) followed by the area code, say 012657 for Ballycastle, followed by the local number. The phone system, North and South in Ireland, is generally very good though public phones in the North are sparse due to non-development of tourism during the Troubles. For phoning out of Ireland, North and South, the most efficient and cheapest way is to use Call Cards which are generally available at newsagent shops and post offices.

Taxis

Taxis or hackneys are most obliging in rural Ireland and can be used to shorten a journey or to go from one area to another. One should enquire locally. Rates are generally approx. £1 per mile and there should be no difficulty about carrying two bikes, passengers and luggage, with perhaps a little difficulty about three or more.

The Grand Tour

Introduction

The Grand Touring Route which is described in this book is a clockwise circular one: Dublin through Wicklow and Wexford into Waterford, South Tipperary, Waterford again, Cork, Kerry, Clare, Galway, Mayo, Sligo, Donegal, Derry, Antrim to Belfast, then the Ards Peninsula and through the Mountains of Mourne to Newry. After Newry the route goes through Louth and Drogheda to the magnificent archaeological sites of the Boyne Valley and on via the ancient Hill of Tara — from where Ireland was once ruled — to finish in Dublin. As the book is aimed at those travelling with full luggage, the routes are kept as close as possible to 40 miles/64 km (longer occasionally on flat days) and overnights are in towns or villages where B & B and other accommodation is usually available. You should consider how to use the suggested route having regard to your time available and your particular desires, especially as the best part of this route is the west coast. If the intervening lowlands can be therefore avoided then so much the better. With this in mind, instead of cycling from Rosslare or Dublin the whole way to the west coast, you might consider taking a train at least part of the way (see Travel to and in Ireland, p. 18).

All routes are given a ★ rating roughly as follows:

★   Not great: boring or traffic heavy (or both), to be done only if necessary.
★★   Good route: good scenery, worthwhile and interesting.
★★★   Great route: very good scenery, location, etc.
★★★★ Premier Cru: exceptional-quality route.

The hills grading on the next page is as follows:
1 Quite flat, no real hills of any worth.
2 Some hills, maybe long and high but not so much as to diminish the enjoyment of a full day's cycling on the described route.
3 Hilly or having a lot of hills, not a mountainous route as such but taking mountain passes as necessary; a full day but not overly strenuous.

List of Grand Tour Routes

Day	Hills	Route	Distance	Quality
1	3	Dublin/Glendalough	30 miles/48 km	★★★
2	1	Glendalough/Courtown	34 miles/54 km	★★★
3	1	Courtown/Wexford/ Rosslare Harbour	38 miles/61 km	★
4	1	Rosslare/Waterford/ Carrick-on-Suir	52 miles/83 km	★
5	2	Carrick-on-Suir/ Clonmel/Lismore	42 miles/67 km	★★★
6	1	Lismore/Mallow	36 miles/58 km	★★
7	2	Mallow/Ballingeary	51 miles/82 km	★★★
8	2	Ballingeary/Glengarriff/ Castletownbere	Various	★★★
9	2	Castletownbere/Dursey Island/ Castletownbere	Various	★★★★
10	3	Castletownbere/Kenmare/ Killarney	51 miles/82 km	★★★★
11	2	Killarney/Cahirciveen	a) 50 miles/80 km	★★★
			b) 40 miles/64 km	★★★
12	2	Cahirciveen/Sneem	32 miles/51 km	★★★
13	2	Sneem/Killarney	a) 34 miles/54 km	★★★
			b) 35 miles/56 km	★★★★
14	1	Killarney/Dingle	31 miles/50 km	★★
15	1	Dingle/Slea Head/Dingle	36 miles/58 km	★★★
16	3	Dingle/Tralee	40 miles/64 km	★★★
17	1	Tralee/Listowel/Kilrush	34 miles/54 km	★
18	1	Kilrush/Lahinch/Doolin	46 miles/73 km	★★
19	2	Circuit of the Burren	Various	★★★
Alt		Doolin/Aran/Rossaveal	Various	★★★★
20	1	Doolin/Kinvara/Galway	50 miles/80 km	★★
21	1	Galway/Clifden	58 miles/93 km	★★★
22	1	Clifden/Westport	a) 41 miles/66 km	★★★
			b) 55 miles/88 km	★★★★
23	1	Westport/Achill	55 miles/88 km	★★★
24	1	Achill/North Mayo	Various	★★★
25	2	North Mayo/Ballina	Various	★★★

26	2	Ballina/Sligo	40 miles/64 km	★★
27	1	Sligo/Donegal	39 miles/62 km	★★
28	3	Donegal/Killybegs/ Glencolmcille	33 miles/53 km	★★
29	3	Glencolmcille/Dungloe	42 miles/67 km	★★★
30	3	Dungloe/Dunlewy/ Letterkenny/Derry	41 miles/66 km	★★★
Alt	3	Dungloe/Doochary/ Letterkenny/Derry	33 miles/53 km	★★★
31	1	Derry/Coleraine/Ballycastle	Various	★★★
32	3	Ballycastle/Larne/Belfast	Various	★★★
33	1	Belfast/Portaferry	40 miles/64 km	★★
34	3	Strangford/Warrenpoint	38 miles/61 km	★★
35	1	Warrenpoint/Clogherhead	52 miles/83 km	★★
36	1	Clogherhead/Boyne Valley/ Dublin	55 miles/88 km	★★★

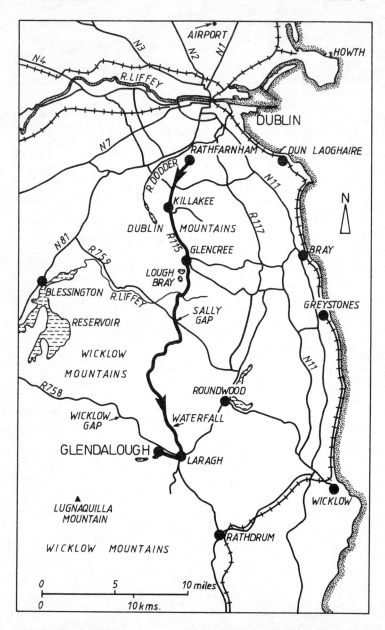

Dublin to Glendalough   ★★★

30 miles/48 km

Description of route: a shorter than average but hilly and lovely route rewarded by super scenery on traffic-free roads to Glendalough, which itself is worth an afternoon at least; try to get there early.

The River Dodder cuts across the south suburbs of Dublin city from west to east. From wherever you are, find the River Dodder, follow it to the bridge between Terenure and Rathfarnham Road. From that bridge go south to Rathfarnham village; then via the Yellow House (public house) follow the signposts or enquire locally for Killakee car park at 1,150 feet. From there head south on the R115/L94 over what are known as the Featherbeds, dropping down to the head of Glencree (IYHA hostel) from where the road rises slowly past Lough Bray. This small but beautiful lake is not visible from the road though can be easily located, being directly behind the only cottage on the right-hand (west) side of the road as you begin to rise out of Glencree. Beyond Lough Bray the road rises steeply until it levels out and a short distance further is a bridge over a stream which is the embryonic River Liffey. A few miles further on Sally Gap is reached: a crossroads in the middle of nowhere. Take the road for Glendalough, perhaps pausing at Glenmacnass Waterfall approx. 6 miles after Sally Gap, but take care as accidents are frequent at this point. After 4 miles Laragh is reached at which turn right for Glendalough (IYHA hostel).

Glendalough itself is worth some considerable time. It has a history going back to the earliest Christian times and was the home of St Kevin, amongst other saints. St Kevin had a little cave or 'bed' — St Kevin's Bed — in the cliff on the west side of the lake but it can only be approached with great difficulty and is to be avoided, since accidents here are frequent. On the east side of the lake there is a track which runs up to the old abandoned lead mines and is an ideal rough camping spot, above which are the Glendalough Cliffs: 300 feet of good granite much beloved by rock climbers.

Recommended lunch stop
Lough Bray or Glenmacnass Waterfall.

✓ For a special treat try Mitchell's Restaurant (and/or B & B) in Laragh. For good value there is an excellent self-service restaurant beside the pub at the bridge also in Laragh.

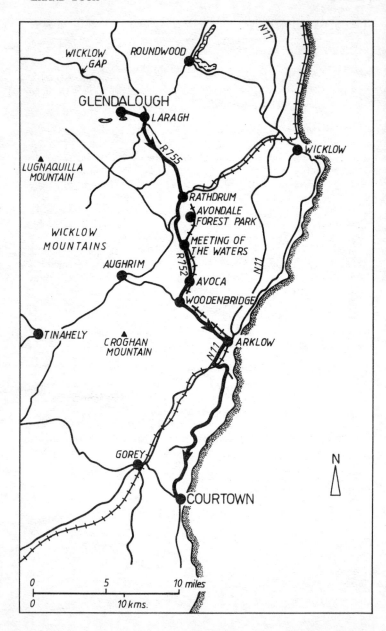

Glendalough to Courtown ★★★

34 miles/54 km

Description of route: a gentle day first through the Vale of Clara followed by the fabled Vale of Avoca then through Arklow to Courtown; a short and possibly lazy day.

From Glendalough go back to Laragh and go right on the R755/T61 for Rathdrum. Ignore the first turn left (in fact it is a parallel road of solitude that could be taken if desired as far as Clara Church), cross Bookeys Bridge and fork left after a few hundred yards. This road, which follows the west side of the Vale of Clara, is a cyclist's delight. Note the church on the valley floor below you halfway down the Vale. If accompanied by children, Clara Lara Funpark, an outdoor adventure park about halfway between Laragh and Rathdrum, is worth a visit. At Rathdrum (IH hostel) you can detour to Avondale Forest Park. Avondale was the home of the famous political leader, Charles Stewart Parnell, and the demesne itself is worth exploring. 1.5 miles after Rathdrum fork left, at which point the road becomes quite busy. Keep on the R752/T7 down the famous Vale of Avoca to Avoca itself, passing the famous 'Meeting of the Waters' on the way. After Avoca is lovely Woodenbridge. Follow the River Avoca to Arklow. Arklow is a thriving small town famous for its pottery and its fishing fleet. Self-caterers are advised to visit the harbour where they may be in luck! There is also a train station on the Dublin–Wexford line. After Arklow take the busy main Dublin–Wexford road (N11) south for 2 miles at which point go left, immediately crossing the Dublin–Wexford rail line for the coast. (If you cross the railway line while still on the main N11 road you have gone too far.) Follow the road 11.5 miles to Courtown, a long-established small seaside resort with good swimming and other facilities.

Recommended lunch stop
Avondale Forest Park.

- ✓ At Avoca attached to the Avoca Handweavers Craft Shop is an excellent restaurant — super quality and reasonably priced.
- ✓ In Lower Main Street, Arklow visit the Stone Oven, a German-owned restaurant and cafe well known for its breads and other produce.

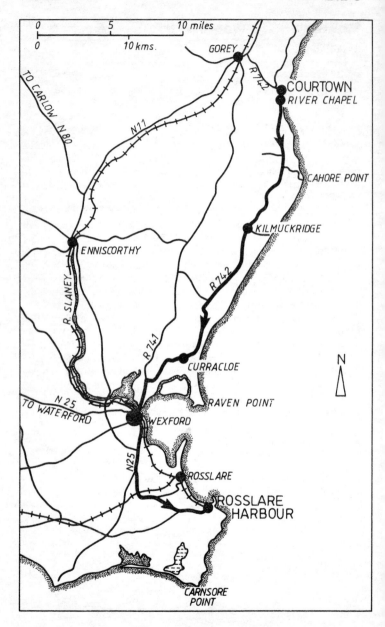

Courtown via Wexford to Rosslare Harbour ★

38 miles/61 km

Description of route: a soft day's cycle, plenty of opportunities for swimming and a chance to see historic Wexford town. Not a great day's cycle, it can be avoided by taking the train from Gorey (4 miles from Courtown) to Wexford and on to Rosslare Harbour if preferred.

Those taking the option of transport by train should take the R742 4 miles to Gorey to the train station. Those cycling to Wexford/Rosslare Harbour should take the coast road through River Chapel. For 20.5 miles to Curracloe this road is a mile or two inland from the coast and at numerous points along the road (Ardamine, Poullshone, Cahore Point, Kilmuckridge and particularly Ballinesker which is a mile north of Curracloe) it is possible to divert a short distance, rarely more than 2 miles, to good clean beaches for swimming. Ballinesker is particularly to be recommended and there is a fine walk from the beach outside Curracloe south 3 miles to the Raven Point, the northern sentinel of historic Wexford Harbour. After Curracloe the road from Courtown (R742/L30A) goes inland 3 miles to a T junction on the R741/L29, at which go left. After 2 miles you enter Wexford town. Some time should be spent here where much of the atmosphere of a mediaeval walled town survives. The town was founded by the Vikings and has a very full history, having been captured from them by the Normans in May 1169 and later by Cromwell's forces. The Maritime Museum is worth at least a short visit.

From Wexford take the main Rosslare Harbour road (N25), following the signs for Rosslare/Rosslare Harbour (IYHA hostel), the former being nearer to Wexford than the Harbour, which is a ferry port having connections with Fishguard, Pembroke, Le Havre and Cherbourg. 7 miles from Wexford town is a left turn on the R740 for Rosslare. The ferry port is straight on from this junction a further 5 miles, still on the N25.

Recommended lunch stop
Ballinesker Beach/Curracloe or Wexford town.

✓ In Wexford town, The Shambles which is located just off the Bull Ring is to be recommended. For mussels, Tim's Tavern in Lower Main Street, Wexford town, is to be recommended.

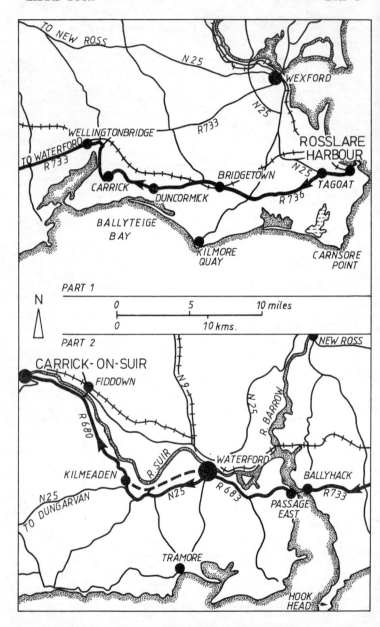

Rosslare via Waterford City to Carrick-on-Suir ★

52 miles / 83 km

Description of route: a flat, nondescript route that would be best avoided by use of the train; not very spectacular but with some rewarding moments, particularly the crossing from Ballyhack to Passage East and the last stage into Carrick-on-Suir.

From Rosslare Harbour (IYHA hostel) take the Wexford road (N25) for 2.5 miles to Tagoat. Go left on R736/L128 through various crossroads to Bridgetown to meet the railway line (train stops here). Follow on R736/L128A through Duncormick and on to Carrick. After Carrick turn right for Wellingtonbridge and main road (R733/L159). Turn left for Wellingtonbridge Station (train stops here). This is now the main Wexford–Waterford road via the Ballyhack–Passage East ferry, so expect traffic. 9 miles further on is Arthurstown (IYHA hostel) then Ballyhack for the ferry to Passage East. The ferry runs backwards and forwards, Passage East to Ballyhack (Arthurstown), continually all day. Both Passage East and Arthurstown are pleasant villages with long seafaring traditions. From the east side of the estuary the R683/L157 into Waterford city can be busy with traffic.

Waterford (IH hostel) is an ancient city which is worth a few hours at least if possible. Because of its location near the mouth of the River Suir and near the conflux of the Rivers Suir, Nore and Barrow it has an extensive history from Viking and Norman times. The events of 1170 and 1171, well documented elsewhere, effectively sealed the course of Irish history for the next 750 years. If time is short then at least Reginald's Tower (on the riverside), erected c. AD 1003 and which is open to the public, should be visited.

After Waterford take the Dungarvan road (N25) for 7.5 miles from Reginald's Tower, then go right on the R680/L26 to Kilmeaden, half a mile. Alternatively a quieter and shorter road is by Mount Congreve (enquire locally) to Kilmeaden. From Kilmeaden take the R680/L26 along the south side of the River Suir for 13 miles to Carrick-on-Suir.

Recommended lunch stop
Ballyhack or Passage East

✓ 5 miles after Wellingtonbridge a short detour brings one to Tintern Abbey — a most impressive ruin, well worth a visit.
✓ In Waterford city the Reginald Pub beside Reginald's Tower is good for pub grub throughout the day.

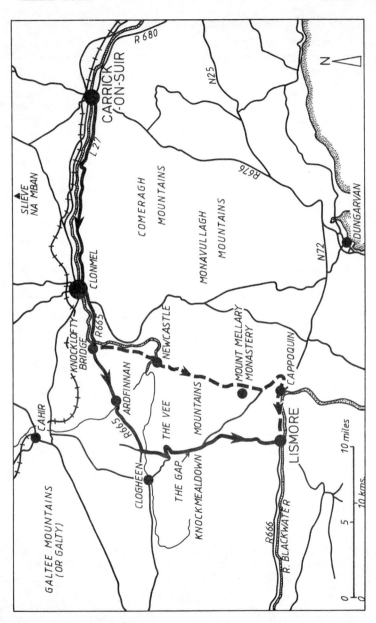

Carrick-on-Suir via Clonmel to Lismore ★★★

42 miles/67 km

Description of route: a delightful run on a secondary road as far as Clonmel on the south side of the river and from Clonmel over the Knockmealdown Mountains by the famous Vee Pass then through one of Ireland's most beautiful glens to picturesque Lismore.

From Carrickbeg on the south side of the river follow the L27 13.5 miles to Clonmel. The slopes to the south of the road are wooded leading up to the Comeragh Mountains and the views to the north are impressive, particularly Slieve na Mban. There are numerous castles and spots for picnicking along the way. The River Suir is at its most beautiful between Carrick-on-Suir and Clonmel, which is a thriving town worth at least a short stop.

From Clonmel follow the R665/L28 south of the river 8.5 miles to Knocklofty Bridge. (Those wishing to forsake the beauty of the Vee for the sanctity of a trip to Mount Mellary Monastery on route to Lismore should go left after Knocklofty Bridge for Newcastle and from Newcastle follow the signposts for Mount Mellary and Lismore.) A boring road leads from Knocklofty Bridge to Ardfinnan, 8.5 miles from Clonmel.

After Ardfinnan continue 6 miles still on the R665/L28 through rolling countryside to a shortcut to the Vee on the left about 1.5 miles before Clogheen at the Crossbar public house.

Turn south for the Vee and head uphill through wooded countryside to The Gap at 1,114 feet. On the way pass Grubb's Grave a little off the road to the left. At this spot Samuel Grubb, one-time owner of Castle Grace, chose to be buried in an upright position. From the top of the Vee it is all downhill to Lismore. 1.6 miles after the top of the pass is a fork; left for Mount Mellary, go right for Lismore. A further 4.4 miles after forking right in a wooded glen is a bridge with a signpost to the left down a slip road to a magnificent picnic site.

Continue down to Lismore passing Glengarra IYHA hostel.

Recommended picnic spot
The Vee or preferably (if making good time) the picnic site on the south side of the Vee as described.

✓ The aptly named Crossbar public house is a very good stopping point.
✓ Try, if at all possible, to visit Lismore's beautiful small cathedral.

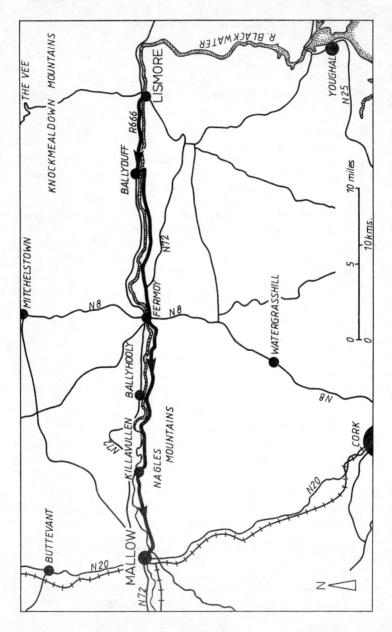

Lismore to Mallow ★★

36 miles/58 km

Description of route: a quiet and dull but never boring cycle, principally along the south side of the River Blackwater with some interesting castles and some fine scenery. This is a short day, enabling you to catch a train from Mallow to Millstreet or Killarney. There are five or six trains every weekday and Sunday is also well served.

Leave Lismore by the R666/T30 going west on the north bank of the River Blackwater. At Ballyduff cross the river to the south bank and go right (west). Follow the River Blackwater to Fermoy.

Leave Fermoy by the main Cork road (N8) and just outside the town go right along the road signposted for Ballyhooly. This road follows the line of the river with good views, particularly after Ballyhooly. Notice the wild garlic along this route on the sides of the road.

Continue on the south side of the river to Killavullen where the castle is worth a visit. Keep on to Mallow still on the south side of the river.

Recommended lunch stop
Fermoy or Ballyhooly.

✓ La Bigoudenne Creperie Restaurant at 28 McCurtin Street, Fermoy is a good French-owned restaurant and well recommended.
✓ The Black Lamb (Sheehan's Bar) and The Georgian Room both in Main Street, Mallow are good stopping places.

Note that it would be preferable if going directly to Killarney to take the train from Mallow to Killarney to avoid that stretch of road. The main road from Mallow to Killarney (N72) is a fast, often narrow, busy main road, quite unpleasant to cycle, and whilst there is an alternative road to the south of the River Blackwater after Millstreet through Caherbarnagh, it is to be avoided at all costs as the road surface is treacherous.

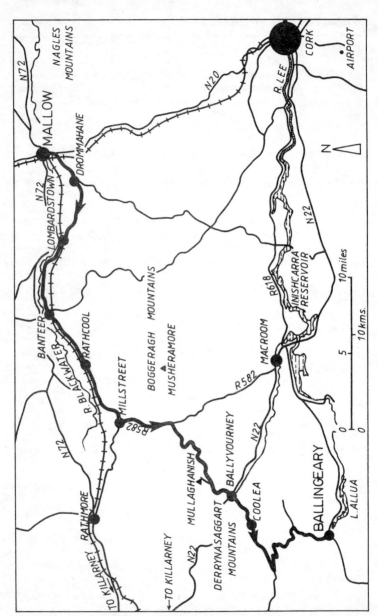

Mallow to Ballingeary   ★★★

51 miles/82 km

Description of route: a varied but tough and demanding day, level at the start but then over two ranges of hills with spectacularly wild and uncrowded mountains on quiet roads.

Can be commenced from Millstreet railway station, 1 mile to the north of the town of Millstreet.

On the south side of the River Blackwater take the R620/L40 3.5 miles to Drommahane then go right for Lombardstown so as to avoid the very busy N72 Killarney road on the north side of the River Blackwater. From Lombardstown go through Banteer and Rathcool to Millstreet. From Millstreet take the R582/L41 3.5 miles to the south on the Macroom road then turn right on to a road which immediately starts rising gradually over a small hill dropping down into a valley. After 1.5 miles there is a fork at which the road obviously goes right, rising gradually and most enjoyably through forestry to cross a small pass after 1.5 miles. The road now drops steeply down past the entrance to Mullaghanish TV mast on the right. At the next junction go left and follow the valley down to join the main road, at which go left for Ballyvourney.

Just beyond The Mills' public house in Ballyvourney is a right turn over a bridge. Take this road for 2 miles to Coolea. 1.5 miles after the village of Coolea there is a bridge on the right, at which keep left and immediately right on third-class road. After almost a mile there is a T junction at which go left. This road rises gradually and then maintains its height before dropping down slightly to a T junction at 2.5 miles. Go right, dropping down a long hill to Ballingeary (IH hostel).

Recommended lunch stop
Definitely The Mills' public house, Ballyvourney; apart from the ambience, the quality of pub grub is well above average.

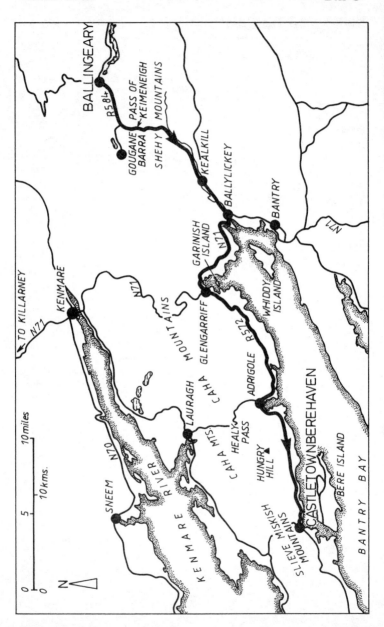

Ballingeary via Glengarriff to Castletownbere ★★★

44 miles/70 km (plus Gougane Barra)

Description of route: a very varied route visiting Gougane Barra, crossing the pass of Keimaneigh before dropping to the sea, then through beautiful Glengarriff and Adrigole to Castletownberehaven (usually shortened to Castletownbere).

From Ballingeary take the R584/T64 for 3.5 miles to a right junction for lovely Gougane Barra. This detour of 2.5 miles into Gougane Barra should not be missed. The forest park and lake are very beautiful and deserve at least an hour or two. Return to the R584/T64 and the Pass of Keimaneigh before dropping down to Kealkill following the Owvane River to Ballylickey. Those wishing to go further south into West Cork go left here for Bantry (IH hostel). Between Kealkill and Ballylickey on the left-hand side are spectacular falls in the River Owvane. Ballylickey is on the sea, and from here to Glengarriff is 8 miles over a road (N71) which rises gradually before falling down into Glengarriff and gives spectacular views of Bantry Bay. If you have time to spare at Glengarriff then Garnish Island (sometimes spelt 'Garinish') is recommended. Take the R572/L61 west from Glengarriff to Adrigole, rising and dropping with spectacular views to the south over Bantry Bay. Adrigole is at the southern end of the high (1,084-ft) Healy Pass. Continue west on the same road which is open and can be windy and busy with traffic (Castletownbere is a very busy fishing port).

Those not wishing to take on the journey to Castletownbere can cut off at Glengarriff for Kenmare (17 miles) or Killarney. The road (N71) rises to cross the Caha Mountains, going through tunnels near the top for this purpose. The road first gives spectacular views back to the south and then having been through the tunnels gives equally spectacular views to the north as it drops down to Kenmare.

Equally, those wishing to visit Bantry and the south-west Cork area should go south (left) at Ballylickey 3 miles to Bantry which can be used as a base for the trips described in the following pages. The route from Bantry or Glengarriff to Killarney via Kenmare would merit ★★★★. If staying in Bantry, then historic Bantry House, a storehouse of art treasures and a very fine Georgian building, is highly recommended for a visit.

Recommended lunch stop
Glengarriff or some lovely spots half a mile west of Glengarriff.

THREE 1-DAY ROUTES BASED ON BANTRY

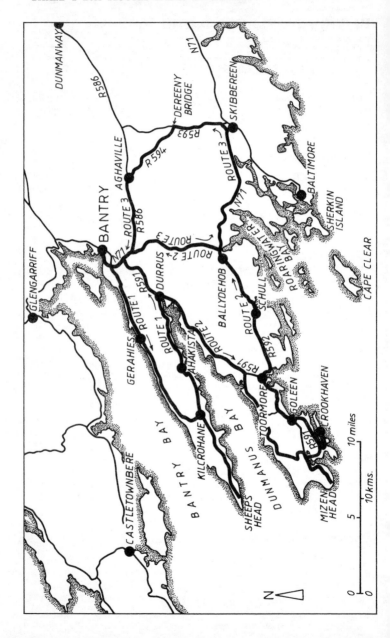

Three 1-day Routes based on Bantry

Route One

Take the south side of Bantry Bay through Gerahies 14 miles to Kilcrohane crossing a 650-ft pass *en route*. From there it is a further 6.5 miles to Sheeps Head which gives very fine views north on a clear day. You should return via the south side of the peninsula (just for variety) through Ahakista, following the R591/L56 back to Bantry.

Total mileage: 42 miles/67 km.
Recommended lunch stop
Sheeps Head.

Route Two

Take the N71 south 2 miles then turn right on the R591 4 miles for Durrus. Follow this road for 8.5 miles; then go right by Dunmanus Castle, keeping to the north side of the peninsula, out to Mizen Head (of weather-forecasting fame). From there visit Crookhaven and then return by the R591 via Toormore, at which point take a right turn for the R592 through Schull and Ballydehob, to rejoin the N71 just after Ballydehob and return to Bantry.

Total mileage: 50 miles/80 km.
Recommended lunch stop
Crookhaven.

Route Three

From Bantry take the N71 south 10 miles to Ballydehob then 10 miles further to Skibbereen. At Hollyhill, 3.5 miles after Ballydehob, you are looking out over Roaringwater Bay to Clear Island (IYHA hostel) which can be reached by ferry from Schull or (more often) Baltimore, which also serves as an overnight stop to make a very good two-day trip based on Bantry. From Skibbereen go directly north on the R593/L59 4 miles to Dereeny Bridge, at which go left on the R594/L60 5 miles to Aughaville to join the R586/T65, from where it is 8 miles to Bantry.

Total mileage: 37 miles/58 km.
Recommended lunch stop.
Skibbereen.

✓ Vickery's Inn is a fine old family-run coaching establishment recommended for accommodation. Almost across the road is the Anchor Tavern which is full of interesting nautical memorabilia — even an anchor.

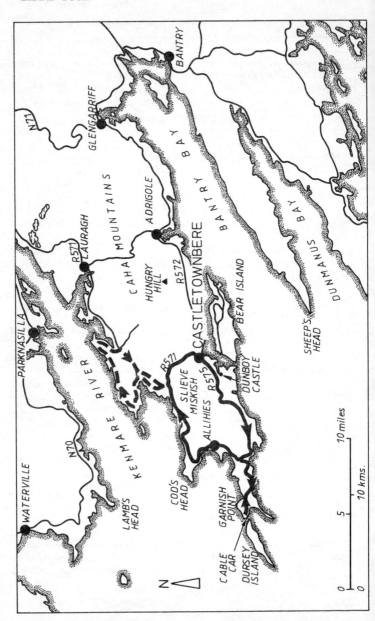

Castletownbere via Dunboy Castle and
Dursey Island to Castletownbere ★★★★

Approx. 40–60 miles/64–96 km, depending on detours

Description of route: a magnificent day of 40–plus miles depending on what is taken in. This route includes historic Dunboy Castle, the cable car at Dursey Island, Dursey Island itself, the beautiful Allihies, the Cliffs of Cods Head and possibly the beautiful Ring of Beara, returning to Castletownbere.

Go west from Castletownbere 2 miles to a signpost for Dunboy Castle, the stronghold of O'Sullivan Beare who fought a guerilla campaign in 1602 against the English following the defeat of the Irish at the Battle of Kinsale. His epic flight to safety in County Leitrim is brilliantly recalled and retraced by Peter Somerville-Large in his book, *From Bantry Bay to Leitrim*. Detour here for the castle and ruined mansion of the Puxley family who formed the basis of Daphne du Maurier's novel, *Hungry Hill*. Return to the main road and follow the R575/L61 west up to about 600 feet before dropping down to a junction signposted left for Dursey Island. Follow this hilly road rising and falling to Garnish (sometimes called 'Garinish' and not, of course, to be confused with Garnish Island at Glengarriff) and the signpost for the cable car to Dursey Island. After visiting Dursey Island (bicycles are not permitted on the cable car) and returning to Garnish go a further 2.5 miles to a T junction, at which go left on the L61A, rising a little before dropping down to spectacular Allihies (IYHA and IH hostel). Follow the road around the coast, rising and falling before dropping down to join the R571/L62, at which you can either go right and over a small pass before dropping down to Castletownbere or continue on 2 miles to a signpost which shows the way around the Ring of Beara, which is a well-rewarded 14-mile addition to the route already described, before returning to Castletownbere. If you have time in hand Bear Island, once a British naval base, is worth a visit. The ferry goes from the pier in the centre of Castletownbere; enquire locally.

Recommended lunch stop
Dursey Island or Allihies.

✓ If possible allow 2 hours plus for Dursey Island. In Castletownbere, McCarthy's and O'Donoghue's pubs are recommended.

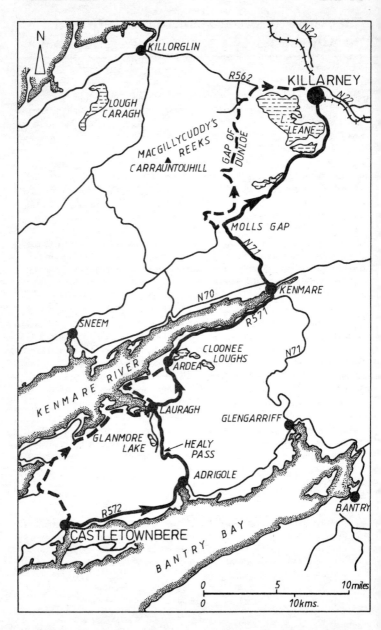

Castletownbere via Kenmare
to Killarney   ★★★★

51 miles/82 km

Description of route: you have a choice of two routes from Castletownbere to Kenmare, depending on fitness. The road directly north from Castletownbere rises to only 350 feet, whereas the Healy Pass to the east rises to 1,084 feet, is very much more spectacular and, therefore, is the one described here. After the Healy Pass the two routes unite through Kenmare and on into Killarney.

From Castletownbere go east on the coast road (R572/L61) 9 miles to Adrigole. At Adrigole go left (north) signposted for Healy Pass and Kenmare and rise almost continuously in a few miles to the top of the spectacular Healy Pass before dropping down first rapidly and then gently into Lauragh, where the easier route is joined. Near here is Glanmore Lake IYHA hostel. From Lauragh you have a choice. The road around the coast stays at sea level and is about 2 miles longer than the main road which crosses a 650-ft pass. Both roads are spectacular and, shortly after they join, Ardea Bridge is reached. On the right are Cloonee Loughs which are freshwater lakes. The road (R571/L62) follows the coast, giving some spectacular views to the north all the way into Kenmare (IH hostel), which is well served with tourist amenities (even a bike shop), having a large number of B & Bs and hotels, including the renowned Park which is rated one of the best hotels in the British Isles.

From Kenmare the N71 road rises spectacularly to Moll's Gap and from there through magnificent countryside but on a busy road by Muckross (IH hostel) and the Lakes of Killarney to Killarney (IYHA and IH hostels). See Grand Tour day 13 for a variation on the straight Moll's Gap–Killarney road.

Note that for those not wishing to take on the Healy Pass the R571/L62 directly north from Castletownbere allows you the bonus of being able to divert from the road on the north side of the peninsula around the Ring of Beara, adding 5 or 6 miles of spectacular coastal scenery. Those wishing to do this should follow the signposts for the Ring of Beara approx. 6 miles after leaving Castletownbere.

Recommended lunch stop
Kenmare.

✓ If stopping in Kenmare, The Purple Heather (which keeps funny hours) is an excellent pub/restaurant — delicious soup and crab! A bit more upmarket is Horseshoe Pub and Restaurant — very highly recommended.
✓ The Bricin is an excellent restaurant (over a book and gift shop) in Killarney's Main Street.

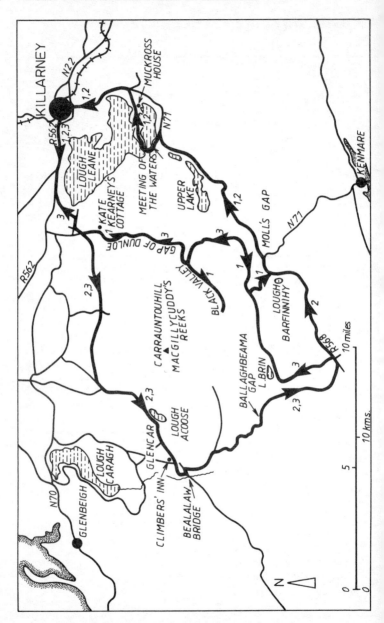

Four 1-day Routes based on Killarney

Four day-long routes for those based in Killarney, the first three in the mountains and the fourth mixing mountains, lakes and the sea.

The first three routes are described going anti-clockwise. At the height of the tourist season there is heavy morning coach traffic going anti-clockwise on its one-day tour of the Ring of Kerry. The routes described here and the coach route part company a few miles outside Killarney. All routes can, equally, be done clockwise. The first three routes require stamina as they are hilly and really only for the cyclist not carrying full luggage. However, it would be very necessary due to the remoteness of the countryside to carry rainwear, repair kit, pump, spare tube, etc. Route One is a shorter, lighter day than Route Two, whilst Route Three is an amalgam of Routes One and Two and involves more climbing. Consider the suggestion at the end of the chapter to make an even more fascinating day tour out of one of the routes. Note that the Gap of Dunloe is best done with a mountain bike. Note also that the Michelin map is misleading in this area. There is a perfectly good road (used in this chapter) along the foot of The MacGillycuddy's Reeks (north side) not shown on Michelin sheet 405.

Route One

3.7 miles   Take the Killorglin road (R562/T67) west from Killarney for 3 miles to a left turn signposted for Kate Kearney's Cottage.

4 miles   Follow signposts to Kate Kearney's Cottage at which point the Gap of Dunloe starts. Note that the first 100 yards or so are usually most uninviting to the cyclist, containing many potholes, excrement, pools of water and mud, etc., but round the first bend things become and remain much better although the road surface is a little difficult until the Black Valley (also known as Cummeenduff Glen) is reached.

6 miles   To the Black Valley through the beautiful and famous Gap of Dunloe. From the top of the gap (a rise of 700 feet from Killarney) drop down steeply to the Black Valley. At this point you can indulge in a little optional extra cycling by going west to the head of the valley, a diversion of approx. 3 miles each way, which on a clear day will reward you with superb views of the Cummeenapeasta Ridge of 3,000-ft peaks to the south of

the valley, running from the top of the Gap of Dunloe across to Carrauntouhill, Ireland's highest mountain. See note at end of Route Three about boating across the Upper Lake.

6 miles   Pass IYHA hostel through some lovely countryside (where the road crosses the river coming down the valley is a good swim spot), to rise 750 feet to Moll's Gap with its nearby Lady's View, regarded by many as one of Ireland's finest viewpoints.

7 miles   Follow the track to Dinis Cottage then continue through the Muckross Estate to the main road to Killarney; but take good care as cyclists are officially encouraged to go the other way!

9 miles   Follow the main road north-east and downhill towards Killarney with some stunningly beautiful scenery to a left turn signposted for the Meeting of the Waters, where you should turn off left for Dinis Cottage to view this beauty spot.

Total mileage: 35 miles/53 km without availing of Black Valley extra mileage. Total climbed: approx. 1,450 feet.

Recommended lunch stop
Swim spot (above).

Route Two

3.7 miles   Take the Killorglin road (R562) west from Killarney (passing Aghadoe IYHA hostel on the right at 2.8 miles) to a left turn signposted for Gap of Dunloe and Carrauntouhill hostel.

1.7 miles   Continue to a T junction and go right.

0.8 miles   Go to crossroads at Dunloe Castle Hotel. Go left to crossroads signposted (west) for Glencar and Carrauntouhill hostel.

10 miles   Go west through a series of crossroads to Lough Acoose which is a beautiful lake set directly below the three peaks of Beenkeragh, Carrauntouhill and Caher. Total rise from Killarney to Lough Acoose approx. 500 feet.

3 miles   To Bealalaw Bridge passing by the well-known Climbers' Inn public house.

5 miles   Just before Bealalaw Bridge turn left then after 300 yards turn right and right again after 1.5 miles to Ballaghbeama Gap rising 800 feet through this magnificent defile.

Four 1-day Routes based on Killarney

5.5 miles   Continue from the top of Ballaghbeama Gap to a T junction at the main road and turn left.

6 miles   Continue east to Moll's Gap by Lough Barfinnihy rising 700 feet.

14 miles   To Killarney as per Route One.

Total mileage for day: 50 miles/80 km. Total rise in height: 2,000 feet.

Recommended lunch stop
Top of Ballaghbeama Gap.

Route Three

28 miles   As per Route One as far as the T junction 5 miles after the Ballaghbeama Gap.

10 miles   Having turned left on to the road for Moll's Gap after half a mile turn left again for Lough Brin, due north. After 3 miles the road turns east rising 650 feet to drop down to the bottom of the Black Valley (note swim spot described in Route One). Continue as signposted to Gap of Dunloe. At this point you have the option of going to the head of the Black Valley (Cummeenduff Glen) adding 6 miles if desired.

12 miles   Ascend 600 feet to the top of the Gap of Dunloe and down the Gap of Dunloe to Kate Kearney's Cottage and back into Killarney.

Total mileage for the day: 50 miles/80 km, plus optional 6 miles/9 km up and down the Black Valley. Total rise in height for the day: 2,550 feet.

Recommended lunch stop
Top of Ballaghbeama Gap or swim spot in Black Valley.

At the bottom of the Black Valley where the river coming down the glen meets the lake, those tourists who have come over the Gap of Dunloe by jaunting car embark by boat to cross the Upper Lake from Lord Brandon's Cottage. Those wishing for a superb ending to a cycling outing might arrange for themselves and their bikes to be taken on a shorter trip across the Upper Lake, an unforgettable outing and one which saves you the need to climb approx. 750 feet to Moll's Gap. Arrangements can only be made with a local boatman by enquiring at Black Valley IYHA hostel.

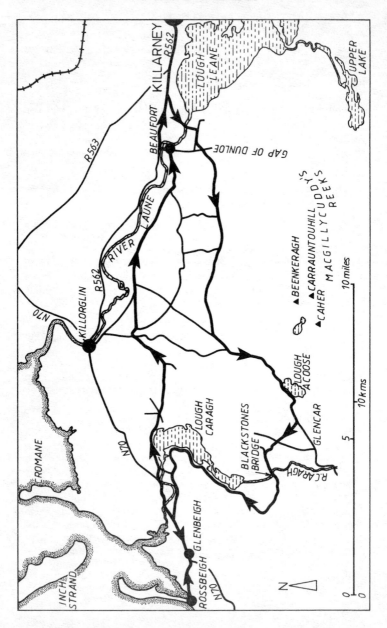

FOUR 1-DAY ROUTES BASED ON KILLARNEY

Route Four

A delightful one-day cycle with superb views of the mountains, a stop by the river and a chance to swim! Careful navigation is required on this route which is a long, enjoyable day (weather permitting) designed to include the mountains, the rivers and the sea with as little interference by traffic as possible. It follows Grand Tour day 11 as far as Glenbeigh.

Go along the Killorglin road to the turn for the Gap of Dunloe. Then take the road along the foot of The MacGillycuddy's Reeks following the signpost for Glencar until Lough Acoose is reached. At Lough Acoose there are superb views of Beenkeragh, Carrauntouhill (Ireland's highest mountain) and Caher, all three over 3,000 feet. From there follow the road for less than a mile to a fork at which go right, following the signposts for Glenbeigh. At just under 2 miles is Blackstones Bridge, which is a superb picnic spot on the River Caragh which flows from Cloon Lough underneath the Mullaghanattin Mountain to Lough Caragh on its way to the sea. After this (recommended stopping point) follow the road along by the west shore of Lough Caragh to reach the main Killorglin–Cahirciveen road (N70) 1.5 miles east of Glenbeigh. From Glenbeigh follow the signs for Rossbeigh which is one of the best-known, safest, cleanest and most beautiful beaches in Ireland, but take care as this is the Atlantic!

Return to Glenbeigh and from there take the Killorglin (N70) road 2 miles to a fork signposting Caragh Lake as 1 mile. (For the next few miles navigation is important.) Take this road (after 100 yards cross the abandoned Killorglin–Cahirciveen railway line) and continue on the north side of Caragh Lake for nearly 3 miles to a junction with five roads. Two main roads are facing; take the right-hand fork (more or less continuing as you arrived) and follow this road for 1.5 miles to a T junction at which go left (north east) for 1.5 miles to a crossroads. Go through this crossroads and after 100 yards the road goes sharply right to meet a bridge after 200 yards, immediately after which go left. From this point the road is bad for almost a mile, after which it joins a road from Killorglin and from this point the road surface improves and the road has superb views for the 5 miles to Beaufort village, at which go left and cross the River Laune to meet the main Killarney–Killorglin R562/T67 road. From here it is 6 miles to Killarney.

Total height climbed: approx. 600 ft. Total mileage: approx. 50 miles/80 km.

Recommended lunch stop
Rossbeigh.

✓ Jack Walsh's Climbers' Inn at Glencar just beyond Lough Acoose is to be highly recommended. It has long been part of Ireland's mountaineering heritage. A short diversion there (to the left at the fork less than a mile after Lough Acoose) will be well repaid.

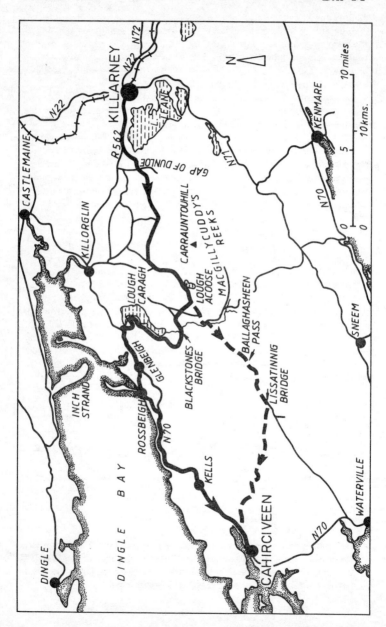

Ring of Kerry: Killarney to
Cahirciveen   ★★★

50 miles/80 km via Glenbeigh
40 miles/64 km via Ballaghasheen

Description of route: a superb day offering a choice of two routes: one peaceful but hilly; the other longer but having the added advantage of enjoying the sea.

Take the R562/T67 Killorglin road for 3.7 miles from the Cathedral to the turn-off for the Gap of Dunloe. Follow the signposts for the Gap of Dunloe until you reach a crossroads close to the gap. Go straight through this crossroads and follow the road (not shown on Michelin sheet 405 but very definitely there, and cycleable!) around the foot of The MacGillycuddy's Reeks until after 16 miles Lough Acoose is reached. This is one of the two starting points most often used in climbing Ireland's highest mountain, Carrauntouhill, 3,414 feet, though not to be recommended unless you are an experienced mountaineer and with proper equipment. Shortly after Lough Acoose is a fork in the road where a choice has to be made:

1. Turn right 1.5 miles to a T junction at which go left to Blackstones Bridge at 1 mile (lovely picnic spot) and then by a beautiful road following signs from Glenbeigh through wooded countryside beside Lough Caragh. This route is lower than Route 2 but after Lough Caragh you are on the main Ring of Kerry road with traffic. From Rossbeigh go 2 miles to spectacular Rossbeigh with one of the most magnificent beaches in Ireland. From Glenbeigh it is 17 miles to Cahirciveen.

Total for the day: 50 miles/80 km.

2. From Lough Acoose go 3 miles to Jack Walsh's Climbers' Inn, public house, shop and hostel-type accommodation. 7.5 miles brings you to Lissatinnig Bridge having crossed the spectacular Ballaghasheen Pass (Oisin's Gap), rising to almost 1,000 feet above sea level. At Lissatinnig Bridge go right at the fork and then a further 10.5 miles to Cahirciveen (IH hostel).

Total for the day: 40 miles/64 km.

Recommended lunch stop
Lough Acoose or anywhere!

✓ The Anchor Bar in Cahirciveen deserves a book of its own. Sadly Pauline Maguire — a well-known playwright — no longer lives, but the pub lives on run by her husband Paddy. A short distance from Cahirciveen is Cooncrome Pier, very good for deep water swimming (enquire locally).

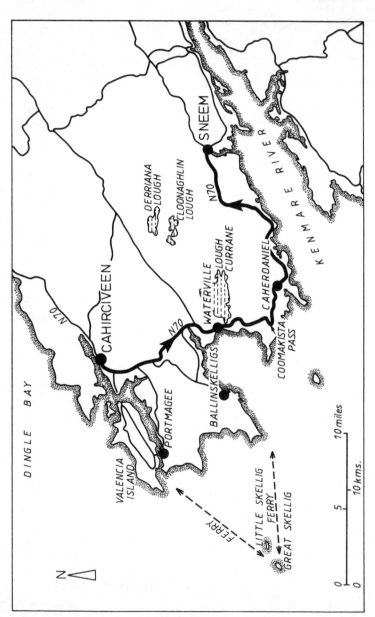

Ring of Kerry: Cahirciveen to Sneem ★★★

32 miles/51 km

Description of route: a short day which allows the cyclist to divert for a trip to The Skelligs.

Go 9.5 miles to Waterville (IH hostel) or Ballinskelligs Bay. Waterville is a picturesque village on the sea. It boasts, a little inland, a first-class hotel (the first Club Mediterranee venture in Ireland) and golf links as well as good fishing at Lough Currane. On the way there is an IYHA hostel at Ballinskelligs, approx. 6 miles off the Ring of Kerry road.

From Waterville it is 9 miles to Caherdaniel (IH hostel) over the Coomakista Pass. The home of Daniel O'Connell, 'The Liberator', which is open during usual hours, is just a little bit off the Ring of Kerry road and is well worth a visit.

From there it is 13.5 miles to Sneem, a picturesque village which boasts a number of good restaurants and B & Bs.

From various points, including Cahirciveen, Portmagee and Waterville, it is possible to take boat trips out to the Great Skellig which is an early Christian monastic settlement on a spectacular rocky island about 8 miles offshore. Together with Newgrange, County Meath and Dun Aengus on Inishmore on the Aran Islands, the Great Skellig would be generally regarded as being one of Ireland's three greatest historic sites. The smaller Skellig is a bird sanctuary on which it is forbidden to land, though it also is a breathtaking sight from the sea. The entire trip, which should not be missed if at all possible, will probably take most of a day and you can only land on the Great Skellig when the sea is not too rough; enquire locally.

Recommended lunch stop
Great Skellig (if at all possible) or Caherdaniel. Derrynane beach, if the weather is any way good, is most definitely worth a visit, being one of the finest beaches in Ireland.

✓ Legendary footballer Michael O'Dwyer has a lively pub in Waterville which serves good pub grub. In Caherdaniel there are two pubs very well worth visiting, An Piobaire Dall (The Blind Piper) and Freddy's.

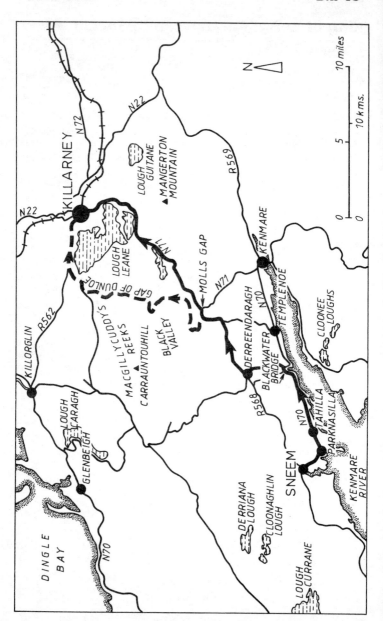

Ring of Kerry: Sneem to Killarney

34 miles/54 km direct
35 miles/56 km via the Black Valley

Description of route: the beauty of this route is such that it creates considerable traffic which can be greatly lessened by taking the R568 from Sneem and then doing Route 2 through the Gap of Dunloe. Nevertheless it must merit ★★★★.

From Sneem keep to the coast road (N70) via Parknasilla and Tahilla 9 miles to Blackwater Bridge, immediately after which take a quiet road to the north 3.5 miles to join the more inland R568. Alternatively, if you are tired of traffic and want a more peaceful journey take the R568 from Sneem 15 miles directly to Moll's Gap through spectacular country. The road leading up to Moll's Gap, and from there to the Muckross Estate on Killarney's Lower Lake, is surely one of the most spectacular sights in Ireland, looking over The MacGillycuddy's Reeks and Carrauntouhill. Half a mile before Moll's Gap there is a choice.

1. A straightforward 15 miles to Killarney through spectacular countryside but with considerable traffic, though at least it is practically all level or downhill.
2. Follow the signs for the Black Valley (IYHA hostel) and having arrived at the Black Valley continue up to the Gap of Dunloe and a further 12 miles to Killarney through the Gap of Dunloe. Care should be taken in the Gap of Dunloe itself — particularly higher up — as the road surface is bad and there are some quite steep sections.

   It is possible at Killarney to save some time by taking the train from Killarney to Tralee (IH hostel). This goes at 16.50 Monday to Saturday, arriving in Tralee 17.25. Tralee is a busy town a little inland from the sea and is the most westerly railway station in Europe in active service.

Recommended lunch stop
Moll's Gap.

✓ A short detour at a junction below Ballaghbeama Gap of approx. 1 mile will lead to the Blackwater Inn which seems dedicated to the memory of a cow that reputedly lived for 48 years.

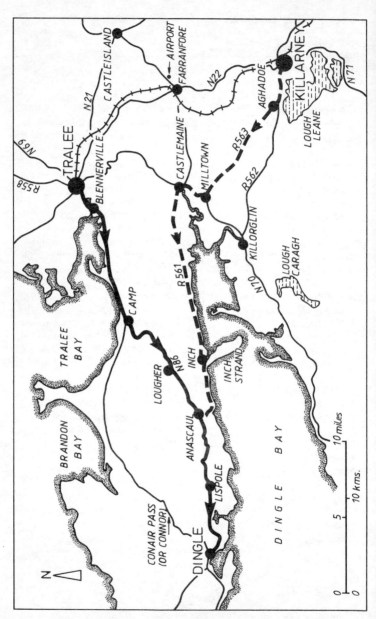

Dingle Peninsula

A tour of the Dingle Peninsula is a magnificent trip, whether for mountaineering, cycling or even just to see Fungi, the dolphin that has become a 'resident' of the area immediately outside Dingle Harbour. The problem from a cycling point of view is that the best part of Dingle is at its western end, so that to get any good 'feel' for the Dingle Peninsula one would want to spend at least three days from Tralee or Killarney and back. The road from Killarney through Castlemaine to Anascaul on the south side of the peninsula is not very rewarding except for Inch Strand (see below). If going to Dingle from Tralee try to ensure that when crossing the Connor Pass you have the best weather — if you have a choice! Note that from Killarney there are three or four trains per day to Tralee so the route to Dingle (Grand Tour day 14) is given from both Killarney and Tralee.

Day One (Grand Tour day 14)   ★★
Day One is recommended for the shorter day, but if the weather is looking good then do Day Three for Day One. From Tralee go to Blennerville and, having crossed the estuary, head west on the N86 9.5 miles to a left turn for Camp. From Camp follow the N86 over a pass rising to 700 feet in the process, through Lougher and drop down to Anascaul (IH hostel) (birthplace and burial place of Thomas Crean, a mere enlisted man who achieved fame with Scott and Shackleton). From Anascaul a worthwhile detour would be to go back 4 miles along the road beside the shore to Inch beach or strand, location of the film *Playboy of the Western World*, the music in which brought Sean O Riada to worldwide public notice for his superb score. From Anascaul it is 11 miles straight to Dingle through Lispole.

Total mileage for day: 31 miles/50 km. Total height: 1,000 feet.

Recommended lunch stop
Inch Strand. Dan Foley's pub in Anascaul should not be missed.

Alternatively, if coming from Killarney the Grand Tour can be linked up with the above route. From Killarney Cathedral go 2 miles on the Killorglin road to the turn-off for the Aghadoe IYHA hostel. This is the R563, which you should follow for a further 8 miles to Milltown, at which take the main Tralee road 2 miles to Castlemaine, home of the Wild Colonial Boy of the famous song. From Castlemaine the R561 takes the south side of the Dingle Peninsula, joining the N86 to Dingle. Approx. halfway is the world-famous 3-mile-long Inch Strand, which is well worth the walk!

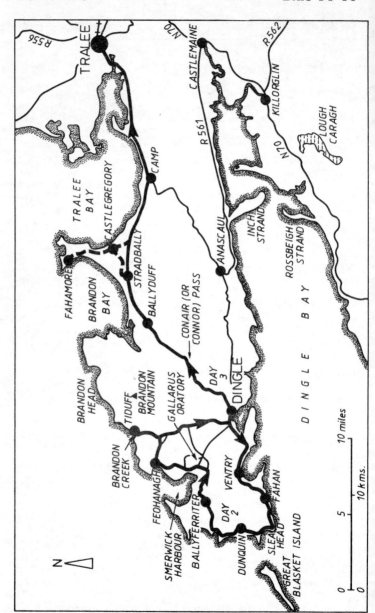

Day Two (Grand Tour Day 15)   ★★★

Go 5 miles west from Dingle to Ventry, then continue further west by Fahan to Slea Head through some remarkably beautiful cliff scenery until the Blasket Islands are in view. If an early start has been made then it is quite possible to get a ferry from Dunquin Harbour to the Great Blasket which is a magnificent excursion. If taken, then allow at least two to three hours to enjoy the island. A walk to its far end is highly recommended. Continue from Dunquin (IYHA hostel) north to Ballyferriter, usually regarded as the most westerly parish in Europe ('next stop America'), and from there further up the coast to the Gallarus Oratory, Smerwick Harbour (IH hostel), Feohanagh and finally to Brandon Creek, beyond which the road does not go. Brandon Creek is directly to the west of Tiduff but not marked on Michelin sheet 405. Return over a 400-ft pass almost directly south to Dingle.

Total mileage for day: approx. 36 miles/58 km. Total height: 500 feet.

Recommended lunch stop
The Great Blasket or Dunquin.

- ✓ Dingle is full of good Irish pubs; T. & G. Ashe and Dick Mac's are the author's favourites, but there are many more! Doyle's seafood pub is one of the best seafood restaurants anywhere in Ireland and is highly recommended for that special occasion!
- ✓ No trip through Dunquin would be complete without a visit to Kruger's Inn — the most westerly pub in Europe and used by the cast of *Ryan's Daughter* when they were shooting the film locally.

Day Three (Grand Tour Day 16)   ★★★

From Dingle take the road over the Connor Pass, reaching a height of almost 1,500 feet in magnificent surroundings. There are spectacular views south across Dingle Bay to The MacGillycuddy's Reeks and north as far as the Mouth of the Shannon. Lough Doon, just north of the top of the pass on the east side, only a few minutes from the road, is recommended for a visit before dropping down to Ballyduff and Stradbally (IH hostel). A diversion here for Castlegregory with its magnificent beach, and Fahamore to the north with its overground graves, adds about 10 miles to the day but is essential. Return to the main road and from there via Camp to Tralee.

Total mileage for day, including Fahamore diversions: 40 miles/ 64 km. Total height: 1,500 feet.

Recommended lunch stop
Castlegregory or Fahamore.

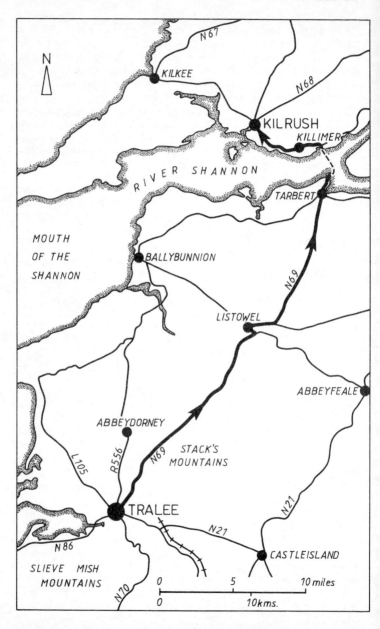

Tralee via Listowel to Kilrush   ★

34 miles/54 km

Description of route: a necessary link between Kerry and Clare which cannot really be avoided except possibly by bus.

Between Tralee and Listowel the road (N69) rises up to 450 feet and presents the cyclist with some fine views to the west. Do not be tempted to take the quieter road (R556/L104) through Abbeydorney or the R551/L105 by the coast to the west. If anything, these are even more boring. Perhaps the route's only saving grace is that, unless you are unfortunate, the prevailing winds will be at your back and good time can be made. There is nothing of note between Tralee and the ferry at Tarbert or worthy of a visit other than Listowel, which is a fine town in which to stop. Listowel is the home town of the distinguished writers Bryan MacMahon and John B. Keane and is also the birthplace of Maurice Walsh and George Fitzmaurice, so that the town's literary tradition in having a Writer's Week each year is well founded. My recommendation is that you put your mind into neutral and your head down until you get to Listowel; enjoy a pleasant stop there and repeat the process to Tarbert. At Tarbert the ferry leaves every hour on the half hour and leaves Killimer on the hour; enquire locally in case of changes in schedules. The journey takes about twenty minutes. Charges for cyclists are modest.

From Killimer take the road to Kilrush which is an enjoyable town worthy of a good overnight stop. Old-fashioned fairs are still held there on certain days and these are well worth enjoying if in the vicinity; enquire locally or phone (065) 53124.

Recommended lunch stop
Listowel or on the Killimer–Tarbert ferry.

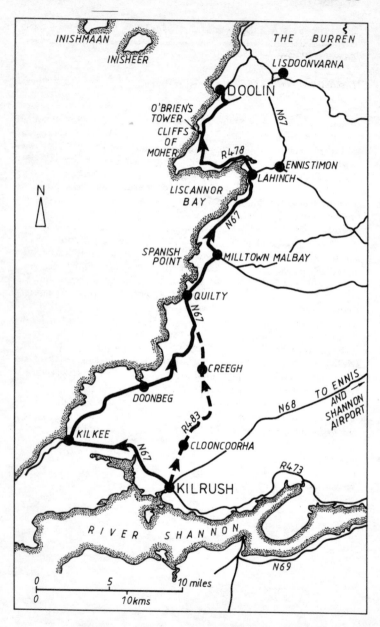

Kilrush via Lahinch to Doolin

46 miles/73 km

Description of route: a fine day's cycling, mostly by the sea, probably with wind behind you and passing the majestic Cliffs of Moher almost at the end of the cycle.

Follow signs N67 8.5 miles to Kilkee which is a long-established holiday resort with good safe swimming. From there follow the N67 road north along the coast through Doonbeg and Quilty by a scenic road to Milltown Malbay, which is the scene of a world-famous festival of Irish piping each year.

Follow the coast road 7 miles further to Lahinch/Liscannor with beautiful sea-cliff views. Lahinch (IH hostel) is not only a wonderful seaside resort just below the Cliffs of Moher, but it boasts one of the best golf courses in the world. Liscannor (IH hostel) is the home of the famous Liscannor flags or slates, much used and admired for flooring and decoration.

Follow the signs for the Cliffs of Moher 9 miles via O'Brien's Tower (a very good place to stop and observe the great variety of seabirds, particularly puffins, on the cliffs) to the turn-off for Doolin, 1.5 miles (follow the signpost). Doolin (IH hostel) is a world-renowned centre for Irish music, and Gussy O'Connor's pub has impromptu Irish music practically every night of the year. In fact, Doolin has often been called the World Capital of Irish music. It is from Doolin Pier that the ferry goes to the Aran Islands, but Doolin itself is worth staying in for two nights: the night you arrive and the night after, because it would be advisable to leave your equipment here and do a one-day tour of the Burren.

Note that it is possible to save a few miles at the start of the day by going directly north from Kilrush through Clooncoorha and Creegh to join the main (N67) road 6 miles south of Milltown Malbay. It is also equally possible to go inland (N68) and spend more time in historic Ennis (IH hostel).

Recommended lunch stop
Milltown Malbay.

✓ Doolin has a number of Independent Hostels and eating places.
✓ The Cloister, Abbey Street, Ennis is a good pub if you are in that town.

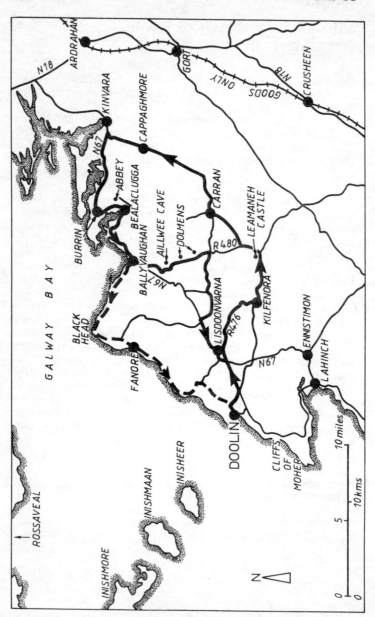

Doolin to Doolin
(Circuit of the Burren)   ★★★

Various 50–55 miles/80–88 km

Description of route: the Burren is such a remarkable area and has such a
concentration of animal and plant life and is so interesting from a historical and
geographical viewpoint that before setting out you should acquire Tim Robinson's
map of the area, which is invaluable as a guide and may well convince you that
the Burren is worth two or more days. The Burren is unique in Europe. It
contains many outstanding features from caves to prehistoric forts and dolmens
and has a fantastic profusion of wild flowers — but be warned! It is strictly illegal
to pick them, however tempting.

This really is a day which gives you a myriad of options. If intending to
continue the Grand Tour by going to Galway city via Black Head then the
following would be recommended: from Doolin, head for Lisdoonvarna,
noting the Spectacle Bridge 1 mile the Doolin side of Lisdoonvarna (IH
hostel). In fact, Lisdoonvarna can be skirted on the R476/L53 to the south of
the town. Continue to Kilfenora, stopping a while at the Burren Display
Centre in Kilfenora and from there still on the R476/L53 to Leamaneh Castle
which is also worth a visit. From Leamaneh Castle go north on the R480/L51
for 1.5 miles then fork right for Carran (or Carron) village which is in the
very centre of the most impressive part of the Burren. From Carran follow
the road first east then to the north east to Cappaghmore (enquire locally),
taking care on the steep descent from the Burren. 4 miles after Cappaghmore
the road running from Kinvara to Burrin village along the shore of Galway
Bay is reached. Take this road left (the main road) and continue around the
coast, first by Burrin village and then by Bealaclugga to Ballyvaughan. If
time permits, a short detour at Bealaclugga to Corcomroe Abbey is very
advisable. It is reached by going south from Daly's public house about 100
yards then left up a bad road. At Ballyvaughan first take the N67 for 1 mile
then go left, following the signposts on the R480/L51 for Aillwee Cave, a few
miles to the south of Ballyvaughan. Aillwee Cave is a commercially
developed cave well worth a visit. From there continue on the R480/L51 to
Poulnabrone Dolmen just off the road on the left (east).

From there it is possible to follow a network of small roads (boreens)
back to Lisdoonvarna and from there to Doolin. Those cyclists following
the Grand Tour via the Aran Islands should return to Ballyvaughan and
then by the coast road around Black Head and Fanore to Doolin directly.

Recommended lunch stop
Ballyvaughan.

✓ Monk's Pub is an imperative!

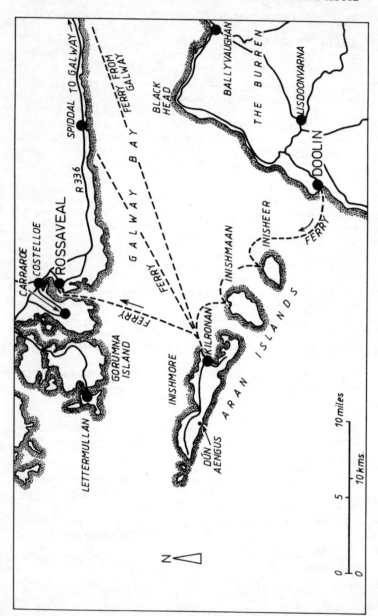

Doolin via Aran to Rossaveal ★★★★

Various

Those going north from Co. Clare into Co. Galway have two choices: either to cycle around by Galway city and from there west to Connemara or to go from Doolin by boat to the Aran Islands and from there to Connemara. In summer, a boat which will take bicycles crosses hourly from Doolin to Inisheer (IH hostel) (1,400 acres/556 hectares), the most southerly of the three islands, subject to demand and weather. The service is less frequent in the off season. The ferry time averages thirty minutes, and having arrived at Inisheer it is possible to continue to Inishmaan (2,252 acres/911 hectares) and Inishmore (7,615 acres/3,082 hectares). From Inishmore there are a number of ferries operating to various parts of Galway, including the city. Probably the most convenient to the cycle tourist is to take the ferry to Rossaveal and from there continue with the Grand Tour. During the summer there are about five sailings per day to Rossaveal from Kilronan and bikes are carried free.

Many hundreds of people visit the Aran Islands each day. The largest number come from and return to Rossaveal, and the most popular is Inishmore, mainly because of Dun Aengus which is acknowledged as one of the finest prehistoric forts in Europe and should not be omitted whatever else is missed.

The islands are a cyclist's paradise, having very few cars and no real hills. On Inishmore the population is about 1,100 persons and 800 bicycles. Some of the latter come with their owners attached but most can be hired by visitors.

Those wishing properly to understand the Aran Islands should purchase Tim Robinson's superb map, Oileain Arann (English text).

July and August are busy times on the Aran Islands, particularly Inishmore — best to enjoy them in May, June or September. A walk along the south sides of any of the three islands is spectacular, but take care! The cliffs can be dangerous and sudden waves have carried off many an unwary person!

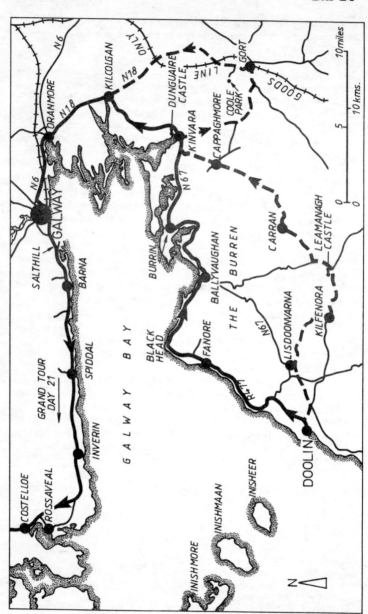

Doolin via Kinvara to Galway ★★

Various 50–55 miles / 80–88 km

Description of route: there are basically two fine routes out of the Burren as far as Kinvara and Kilcolgan, after which it is a busy main road to Oranmore and an even busier main road into Galway city. However, the delights of Galway make the journey worthwhile as Galway would have to rank as one of the finest (if not the finest) towns or cities in Ireland. If you have spent some time in the Burren then this is an opportunity to take an alternative route out of the Burren so as to avoid duplication.

From Doolin either head north for Fanore on the R477/L54 and around Black Head to Ballyvaughan, following the coast through Burrin/Burren village to picturesque Kinvara (IH and IYHA hostels) with its lovely Dunguaire Castle 33 miles from Doolin. Just before Kinvara the main alternative route from Doolin via Lisdoonvarna, Leamaneh Castle, Carran village and Cappaghmore is joined. After Kinvara follow the N67 6 miles to join the main N18 road from Ennis to Oranmore and Galway at Kilcolgan. If you have time to spare, Morans of the Weir, a beautifully situated public house specialising in oysters and seafood, is a short detour to the west off the main N18 road a little to the north of Kilcolgan — follow the signposts — and is to be recommended. After Kilcolgan follow the busy main road 5.5 miles to Oranmore where it joins the main N6 Dublin–Galway road for a further very busy and unavoidable main road 5.5 miles to Galway city (IH and IYHA hostels). It is possible at Kinvara to go across country to the south east to famed Thoor Ballylee, site of Yeats Tower which was once the residence of William Butler Yeats, Ireland's national poet, and adjacent to Coole Park where there is a famous tree on which are carved the initials of well-known writers and artists including those of Shaw, O'Casey, W.B. Yeats, Jack B. Yeats and AE (George Russell). This is a little out of the way but would certainly reward the adventurous cyclist as it would afford the opportunity of seeing the small town of Gort, the ancestral home of Lord Gort of World War I fame.

Recommended lunch stop
Kinvara or (preferably and if making good time) Morans of the Weir.

✓ There is a nice coffee shop in the small square in Kinvara.

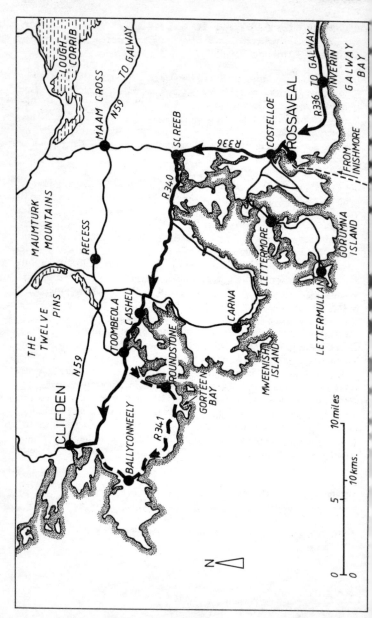

Galway to Clifden   ★★★

58 miles/93 km (add 10 miles/16 km for Roundstone diversion)

Description of route: this is a long day. It is 58 miles by the main road to Clifden and 68 miles following the coast to Roundstone. It is not advisable to go from Galway to Clifden on the N59 because the stretch of road between Galway city and Oughterard is very busy and quite narrow at spots and therefore quite unpleasant at times for cyclists. The coast road is better, though with more traffic than most of the routes in this book, and is preferable even though a few miles longer.

From Galway city follow signs for Salthill, an attractive seaside resort which has retained its popularity when many other seaside resorts have faded. Enjoy a swim in the sea here on a fine day. From Salthill keep on the coast road to Barna and Spiddal through Inverin (IYHA hostel) to Costelloe where those taking the Alternative Route from Doolin via Aran to Rossaveal rejoin us. As far as Spiddal and beyond is a classic example of ribbon development — bungalow after bungalow — but at least it is by the sea. Those who want to dally a while should consider a tour of the peninsula and islands to the west: Lettermore, Gorumna, Lettermullan, etc. From Costelloe it is 13.5 miles to Lettermullan, going from island to island by causeway, and as it is flat it is a very rewarding journey though almost inevitably breezy. From Costelloe rejoin the Grand Tour and continue for Clifden (IH hostels) approx. a further 30 miles. It is possible to do the trip from Galway to Clifden in one day (58 miles/93 km).

This is a long day by the standards of this book, but since the terrain is quite flat consideration should be given to taking the southward diversion for Roundstone on the R341/L102. The extra 10 miles of cycling is rewarded with some spectacular scenery.

Recommended lunch stop
Anywhere past Costelloe.

✓ Even if not going through Roundstone it is worth making a small diversion to view this picturesque village and enjoy a drink and/or quality pub grub in O'Dowd's pub overlooking the harbour.

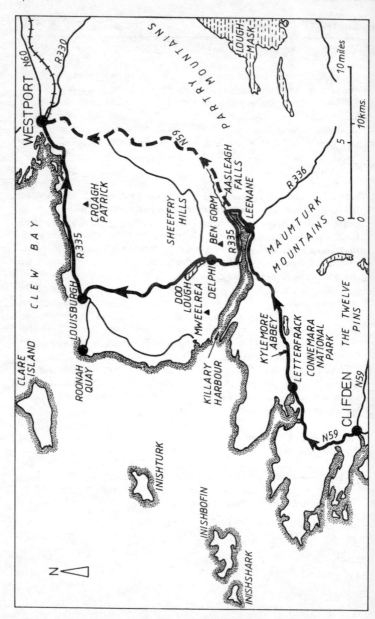

Clifden to Westport

direct to Westport   ★★★
via Doolough   ★★★★

---

41 miles/66 km direct
55 miles/88 km via Doolough

Description of route: a long day but with no great climbing and if taken through Doolough probably the finest day's cycling in Ireland.

From Clifden take the main N59 north following Westport signs, first to Letterfrack (IH hostel), where the national park is worth a visit. Equally, the restaurant, craft shop and the abbey itself at Kylemore Abbey is worthy of a stop, after which comes some lovely lakeside cycling to Killary Harbour and Leenane (the setting for the much-acclaimed film, *The Field*). Leenane is at the head of Killary Harbour, once reputed to be one of the only two places in the British Isles capable of taking the entire British Fleet. Ten ships of the Channel Squadron visited there for some time at the end of October 1899 (*Majestic*, the flagship of the fleet, had as a young Torpedo Officer Robert Falcon Scott, later to achieve fame as Scott of the Antarctic). 1.5 miles past Leenane the R335/L100 goes to the left. The main road continues 17 miles to Westport through pleasant rolling countryside with fine views. The more adventurous should go back along the north shore of Killary Harbour past the beautiful Aasleagh Falls on the R335/L100 for 3 miles to where the road goes between the Mweelrea Mountains and Ben Gorm/Sheeffrey Hills. After 1.5 miles Delphi is passed and then Doolough, after which the road rises over a low pass to reveal, on a fine day, stunning views of the Atlantic with Inishturk, Clare Island and Achill to the west/north west. The road continues to Louisburg and then runs 13 miles along the south shore of Clew Bay — reputed to have 365 islands — under Croagh Patrick (Ireland's most sacred mountain and a place of pilgrimage climbed barefoot by many penitents every year) into Westport (IH and IYHA hostels). Westport itself is a purpose-built and beautiful town — 'a great place for the craic'. Around Westport Quay are to be found The Asgard and Quay Cottage, both excellent establishments, whilst in Westport itself Matt Molloy's (of Chieftains' fame) is renowned for its Irish music.

Recommended lunch stop

At the little harbour just as one leaves Killary Harbour itself to go north between the mountains, or at Doolough.

- ✓ Jimmy Somerville's The Bards Den does good pub grub.
- ✓ For a real treat the journey could be broken overnight at Portfinn Lodge, Leenane. This establishment offers truly excellent hospitality, very reasonably priced and with some of the best seafood in Ireland.

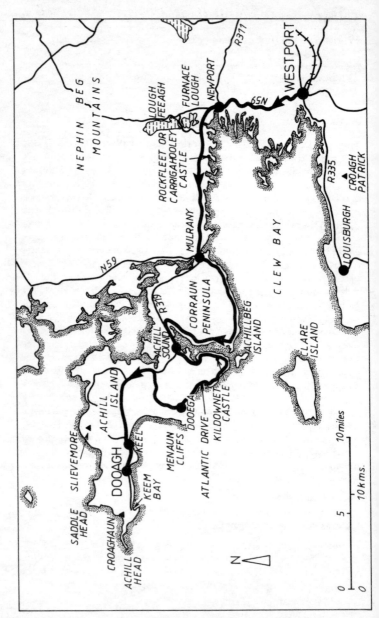

Westport to Achill (Dooagh)   ★★★

55 miles/88 km (not including Rockfleet Castle)

Description of route: a lovely mixture of sea, islands, cliffs and scenery to Dooagh, the most westerly village on Achill Island, via the famous Atlantic Drive.

Take the N59 to Newport and then Mulrany. 3 miles after Newport take a detour to the left to Carrigahooley (or Rockfleet) Castle which should not be missed. In 1574 Grace O'Malley beat off an English attack here. Further along the way notice evidence of the now-defunct railway line to Achill Sound. At Mulrany turn left (south) to take the coast road around Corraun Peninsula, 12.5 miles to Achill Sound. Cross Achill Sound and again turn left to keep the Sound itself on your left as you go south down the Sound to Kildownet Castle (which is also associated with the famous sea-queen, Grace O'Malley) and the harbour at the southern tip of the island opposite Achillbeg ('Little Achill') Island, before turning back north west along the famous Atlantic Drive to Dooega. From Dooega return to the R319/L141 which is the main central road on Achill Island and go 4 miles to Keel (IH hostel) and a further 1 mile to Dooagh, which was the home of Captain Boycott, whose name gave that word to the English language.

A trip a further 2 miles to Keem Bay (a beautiful beach in a beautiful setting) ought to be taken in if at all possible. From Keem Bay the intrepid walker can go to Achill Head but only with great care as the cliffs are high and treacherous! In fact, Achill is worth a day at least on its own for the cycle tourist or walker.

Recommended lunch stop
Atlantic Drive or the harbour opposite Achillbeg Island.

- ✓ Newport offers a choice of two excellent establishments both serving pub grub: the Anglers Rest at the top of the Main Street and Chambers a little further on on the right. Apart from this there is very little until you are well into Achill.
- ✓ There are not many eating places in Achill but outstanding amongst them is The Chalet at Keel.

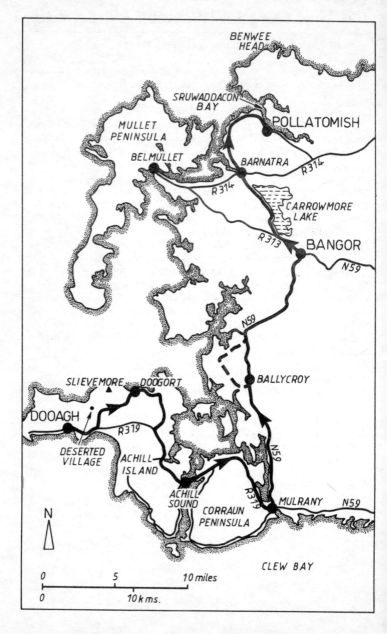

Achill to North Mayo   ★★★

Approx. 40–56 miles / 64–90 km

Description of route: a lovely long but flat day, hopefully with the benefit of the prevailing winds over the quiet and peaceful roads of West Mayo.

Note that the route envisages stopping soonest at Bangor, a small town with available accommodation, or latest at Pollatomish IYHA hostel further to the north, both being ideally located for Day 25, the rugged coastline of North Mayo. Note also that an alternative to going all the way to Ballina on the following day is to overnight at Killala (the location of *The Year of the French*), a historic and scenic town 7.5 miles north of Ballina on the described route to Ballina.

From Dooagh return to the mainland firstly by way of the Deserted Village under Slievemore then by Doogort and the north side of the island to Achill Sound. From Achill Sound take the north side of the Corraun Peninsula to Mulrany (noticing many signs of the abandoned railway line linking Westport with Achill Sound), at which point rejoin the N59 signposted for Bangor. The road from here to Bangor is flat and quiet allowing detours if desired (enquire at Ballycroy — 9 miles after Mulrany — for the location of *The Ballroom of Romance*, an acclaimed TV production). Accommodation is available in Bangor or you can continue to the IYHA Hostel at Pollatomish a further 14 miles by the recommended (and much flatter) route going up the west side of Carrowmore Lake and then following the sea shore north and around into Sruwaddacon Bay to the hostel.

Recommended lunch stop
Mulrany.

✓ So far as can be ascertained this is a gastronomic desert with little or no oasis in sight! However, if going to Belmullet (and a detour to take in the Mullet Peninsula is highly recommended) the author recommends the Western Strands Hotel in Main Street, Belmullet, a small family-run hotel giving excellent value for simple accommodation, with good food.

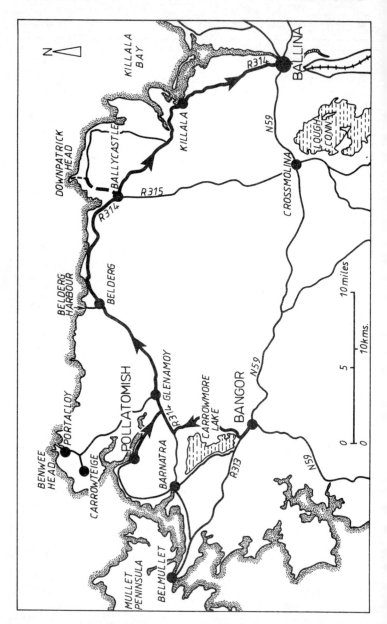

North Mayo to Ballina　　　　★★★

Approx. 40 miles/64 km

Description of route: this should be a great day on quiet roads affording the opportunity to explore the wild and very impressive cliffs of the North Mayo coast.

Note that many would consider that the Mullet Peninsula and also the Carrowteige/Portacloy area (the latter being a genuine Gaeltacht or Irish-speaking area) are each worth at least a day's exploration, and serious walkers with OS sheet 6 will note the obvious line of sea cliffs from Benwee Head east to Belderg Harbour. Note also the suggestion made in day 24 about overnighting in Killala.

From either Bangor or Pollatomish get to the R314/L133 and go east to Glenamoy, then follow the Glenamoy River rising gently to about 250 feet before dropping down to Belderg, at which point the best part of the day begins. Continuing east the road rises to 400 feet above the sea on a very scenic 10-mile stretch to Ballycastle. After Ballycastle a detour to the north to Downpatrick Head should not be missed even though the last mile has to be walked. This headland is made more dramatic by Doonbriste, a detached sea-stack, and by a number of extraordinarily impressive puffing holes — but be careful, there have been many fatal accidents here!

After Downpatrick Head continue either to Ballina (IH hostel) or stop at historic Killala (IYHA hostel), the choice being between a busy town with the usual amenities and a small town steeped in history, peace and quiet, respectively.

Recommended lunch stop
Downpatrick Head.

✓ There is very little in the way of sustenance to be had between North Mayo and Ballina (or at least Killala) except at the Ceide Fields where the journey could be broken. This recently opened Interpretative Centre is one of the best of its kind in the country. It deals with a time going back 5,000 years when this part of the country was heavily populated. There is a coffee shop at the centre.

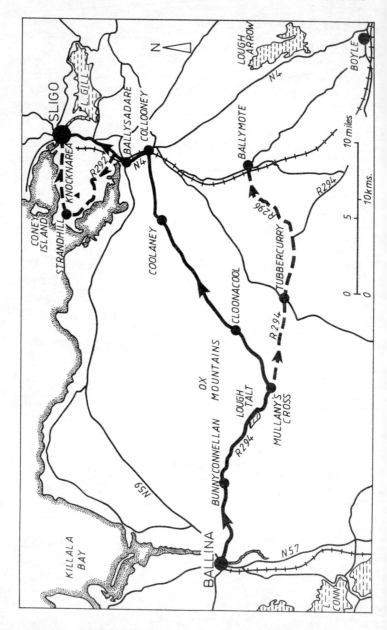

Ballina to Sligo   ★★

40 miles/64 km

Description of route: a very good route with a superb first half perhaps losing a little quality in the latter stages but allowing one to connect with an evening train to Dublin, thereby giving a full day's cycling and ending up in the capital city if not continuing on into Donegal.

From Ballina take the R294/L133 east through Bunnyconnellan gradually rising into the Ox Mountains to a height of 700 feet to a point overlooking Lough Talt. This is the best part of the day. From Lough Talt the road drops down to Mullany's Cross where the road forks left (north east) away from the main road and along the base of the Ox Mountains by Cloonacool and Coolaney on a very enjoyable and quiet road to Collooney. From Collooney one can go north on the main Dublin–Sligo (N4) road 7 miles to Sligo (IYHA and IH hostels) or catch an evening train 18.29 to Dublin (weekdays) or 18.10 (Sundays).

An interesting detour which adds approx. 5 miles of very interesting and scenic countryside is as follows: after Collooney go 2 miles on the Sligo road to Ballysadare and approx. half a mile after Ballysadare go left on the R292/L132 signposted for Strandhill. Follow the signposts around until after 4 miles you are under the Cliffs of Knocknarea which are very impressive. This small (1,078-ft) hill can be climbed quite easily and with no danger from a point on the east side. Continue on around to Strandhill, which is a favoured seaside place for the surrounding counties and looks out on Coney Island! Follow the road east from there to Sligo town.

Note that the nearest railway station to Ballina on the Sligo–Dublin line is at Ballymote which is reached by following the main road from Lough Talt through Mullany's Cross into Tobercurry (sometimes Tubbercurry) and then by turning left off the Tobercurry–Boyle road (R294/L133) 4 miles after Tobercurry on the R296/L151 — a saving of almost 10 miles on the distance to Boyle. Trains leave Ballymote at least three times daily (enquire locally), arriving Dublin approx. three hours later.

Recommended lunch stop
Lough Talt.

- ✓ Tobercurry is an interesting small Irish town. Killoran's pub is recommended for food but even more for the entertainment and the huge amount of memorabilia around the walls.
- ✓ Hargadons pub in O'Connell Street in the centre of Sligo is a superb example of the best in the Irish pub tradition.

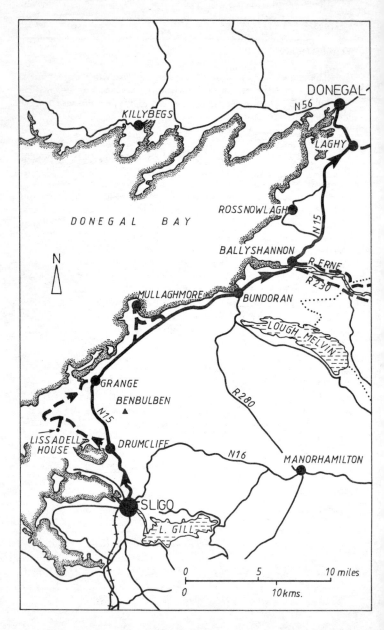

Sligo to Donegal   ★★

39 miles/62 km

Description of route: an interesting day on a flat and busy main road with fine sea views to the west and some wonderful views of Benbulben to the east.

Leave Sligo town by the main Donegal (N15) road and go 4 miles to Drumcliff, an important early Christian monastic site founded by St Colmcille in AD 575. At Drumcliff pause a while at the grave of William Butler Yeats, Ireland's national poet, on whose tombstone are carved the immortal words: 'Cast a cold eye on life, on death, Horseman pass by.' Immediately after Drumcliff if you have some time to spare you should visit Lissadell House to the west of the main road, a detour which will enable you to rejoin the main road at Grange having only cycled an additional 5/6 miles. The Lissadell Estate is a Forestry and Wildlife Park, famous as a winter refuge for the barnacle goose which comes here from Greenland. The bay has many seals that can be seen basking on offshore sandbanks. Lissadell House is worth a visit. It belonged to the Gore-Booth family, which included Sir Henry Gore-Booth, the arctic explorer, and his daughters Eva, the poetess, and Constance, later Countess Markievicz, the first woman elected to a seat in the British House of Commons. After Drumcliff the road continues north and then north east so that if the prevailing winds are behind you the cycling can be a real pleasure. 9 miles after Drumcliff is a left turn on the R379 to Mullaghmore, a tidy village with a scenic castle. It was in Mullaghmore Bay that Lord Louis Mountbatten was tragically assassinated. Rejoin the main road and almost immediately enter County Leitrim, which has a 3-mile coastline, after which comes Bundoran (IH hostel), a very popular seaside resort over a long number of years. After Bundoran the road loses interest as it goes through Ballyshannon (IH hostel) to Laghy which is only 3 miles from Donegal town (IH hostel). Those wanting to enjoy a good beach can do so almost anywhere along this coast, though the beach at Rossnowlagh is very highly regarded; follow the signs to the west (left) after Ballyshannon. The last 3 miles into Donegal town give pleasant sea views.

Recommended lunch stop
Mullaghmore.

✓ A detour at Ballyshannon for 4 miles brings one to Smugglers Creek, a delightfully located pub/restaurant/B & B of excellent quality and value situated in a prominent position looking over the beautiful Rossnowlagh Strand. A half day and an overnight here would amply repay those with a little time to spare.

✓ The Bridge Bar on the main street in Bundoran does good pub grub.

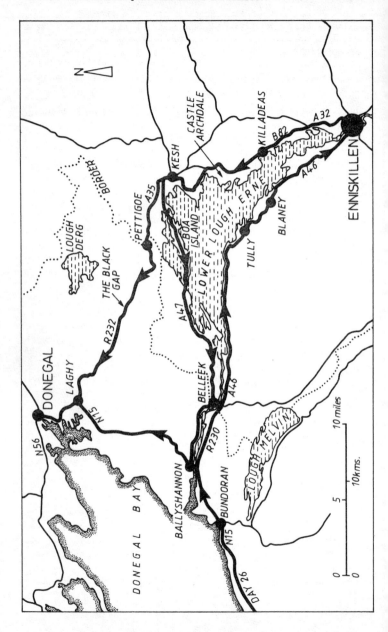

2-day Enniskillen/Lough Erne Diversion

Instead of Grand Tour days 26 and 27, an alternative is to take three days Ballina to Tobercurry and Boyle or Lough Key (overnight), Drumshanbo, Blacklion, Enniskillen (overnight); Castle Archdale, Pettigoe, Laghy/Donegal town to connect up with the Grand Tour. For a further variation, Grand Tour day 27 can be made into two days taking in Enniskillen, both days being longer than average but with no great hills to contend with, as follows:

Day One
Take Grand Tour day 27 for 26 miles via Bundoran to Ballyshannon. Do not cross the bridge into Ballyshannon but continue straight on the R230/L24 for the Border. Just at the Border there is a left turn for Belleek across the River Erne which is worth a short stop, being the home of the famous Beleek china. Keep on the south side of the river now on the A46 along the south side of Lough Erne via Tully (where Tully Castle, a fortified house with seventeenth-century-style gardens, can be visited) and Blaney to Enniskillen, which is 34 miles from Ballyshannon; total 60 miles for the day. This is longer than the average, is fairly flat and is a very pleasant cycle, mostly by the lakeshore. Enniskillen itself is a pleasant town with some lovely old-style public houses.

Day Two
From Enniskillen go north on the east side of Lower Lough Erne, first on the A32 for 3.5 miles to a fork, at which go left on the B82 which follows the east side of Lower Lough Erne, passing St Angelo Airport and through Killadeas to an entrance to Castle Archdale Country Park and Forest (YHANI hostel) at 6.5 miles. It is possible — indeed recommended — to go through Castle Archdale Country Park without the loss of too much time and to rejoin the B82 which continues to Kesh. Less than 1 mile after Kesh the road forks. The right fork goes directly to Donegal town via Pettigoe first by the A35 and then, having crossed the Border back into the Republic, across the Black Gap rising to 600 feet on the R232/T35 to Laghy and Donegal town. The better but longer route goes left at the fork described just north of Kesh and follows the A47 along the north shore of Lower Lough Erne. Just over 2 miles after the fork the road crosses Portinode Bridge and then traverses the full length of Boa Island where, after 5 miles, at Iniskeeragh there is a two-faced Celtic idol in Caldragh Cemetery and then to the 'mainland', to follow the north shore of Lower Lough Erne to Belleek. At Belleek turn right and a short distance north of Belleek go left and follow the north shore of the River Erne 3.5 miles to Ballyshannon and from there continue Grand Tour day 27.

SIX SHORT TOURS FROM ENNISKILLEN

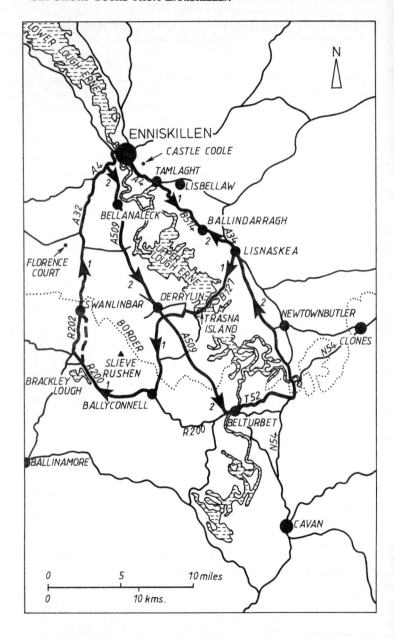

Six Short Tours from Enniskillen

In all of Northern Ireland Enniskillen is probably the best centre as a base for a cycling holiday. Apart from the amenities of the town itself and the other non-cycling activities available, both water and land based, the surrounding countryside gives ample scope for short and long one-day tours.

Apart from the circuit of Lower Lough Erne described as a diversion from Grand Tour day 27 the following five tours are a good representative sample, though they are by no means all that are available.

If cycling in this area large-scale maps are recommended, as the smaller-scale maps (Michelin, etc.) do not contain all the roads described or otherwise available to the cyclist.

Note that due to the proximity of Enniskillen to the Border between Northern Ireland and the Republic of Ireland it is necessary on some of these routes to cross that Border. Care should be taken to observe road signs, instructions, etc., and delays may also occasionally be experienced.

1. Circuit of Slieve Rushen

From Enniskillen take the A4 Lisbellaw road south from Enniskillen on the east side of the River Erne for 3 miles to a junction. This first 3 miles is a scenic foretaste of the beauty of the Erne Waterways and on the way you pass (on the left) Castle Coole, a perfect example of eighteenth-century Hellenism built for the Earls of Belmore. After taking the right turn at the junction continue through pleasant cycling country a little away from Upper Lough Erne until after 7 miles Lisnaskea is reached. At Lisnaskea turn right on the B127 and after 4 miles cross the Erne via Trasna Island and two bridges. 2 miles further the main Belturbet–Enniskillen road (A509) is reached. Cross this and continue around the side of Slieve Rushen 6 miles to Ballyconnell having crossed the Border 1 mile before the town. At Ballyconnell the canal connecting the Erne and the Shannon waterway systems is briefly joined. After Ballyconnell continue first on the R200/L50 then on the R202/T53 10 miles to Swanlinbar, a small town just south of the Border on the main Ballinamore–Enniskillen road. It is possible to avoid the main road but a one-inch map or equivalent would be necessary to avoid getting lost. Cross the Border north of Swanlinbar and continue 12 miles to Enniskillen. Note that 3 miles north of the Border on the left there is a road leading to an entrance to Florence Court which is a magnificent stately home, being the family seat of the Earls of Enniskillen; seasonally open to the public. From there it is 6 miles to Enniskillen. Total mileage approx. 44 miles/70 km.

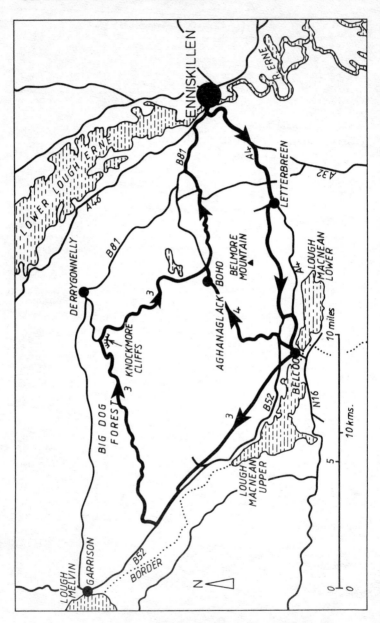

2. Circuit of Upper Lough Erne

This is a boring route at the start which may not even be possible to cycle because the (British) Army has blocked the road at a bridge below Derrylin connecting the Republic with Northern Ireland. However, it should be possible for a cyclist wheeling a bike. The route improves in the latter half.

Take the main A4 road leaving Enniskillen to the south west for 1.5 miles to a left-hand turn on to the A509, then a further 3.5 miles to Bellanaleck and a further 8 miles to Derrylin. After Derrylin still on the A509 continue a further 6 miles to the Border, which is the Woodford River at this point and which should be passable to cyclists wheeling bikes. Having crossed the Border into the Republic continue to the Ballyconnell–Belturbet (R200/L50) road at which go left and having crossed the River Erne enter Belturbet.

After Belturbet take the T52 (signposted Clones 12) on a road of potholes 4.1 miles east to join the Cavan–Clones main road (N54). Go left on this road to reach the Border, after half a mile crossing back into Northern Ireland and from there a further 0.8 miles to a junction at which the main road goes right to Clones. Continue straight (ignoring the right turn for Clones) for a further 0.8 miles to a permanent (British) Army checkpoint and a further 0.6 miles to a fork, at which the main road goes right for Newtownbutler and the minor road goes left (signposted Crom 5), a quiet road near the lake. Unless you need to go by Newtownbutler it is best to keep to the left road which brings you after 8 miles of extremely pleasant cycling through open rolling farmland to Lisnaskea. At Lisnaskea the A34 is joined for a short distance. 1 mile after Lisnaskea at a roundabout go left on the B514 through Ballindarragh to arrive at the A4 near Tamlaght after 7.4 miles. After this it is 2 miles of scenic road to Enniskillen. Total mileage approx. 47 miles/74 km.

3. Big Dog Forest and Back

This is a hilly but very enjoyable route and is highly recommended, being probably the finest day route from Enniskillen described in this chapter.

Take the A4 road south west from Enniskillen to Belcoo at 12 miles. The latter part is on a scenic road at the foot of Belmore Mountain above Lough Macnean Lower. In fact, at Letterbreen, 5 miles from Enniskillen, it is recommended to go right (north) and almost immediately left (west) on to a third-class road which runs parallel to the main A4 road at a higher, more scenic level to rejoin the A4 2 miles before Belcoo. This highly recommended secondary road is immediately quite hilly but the effort is amply repaid and having gained height remains very enjoyable all the way. From Belcoo continue on the B52 for 1.5 miles to a four-road junction and take the road signposted 'Scenic Route'. This road also rises but, again,

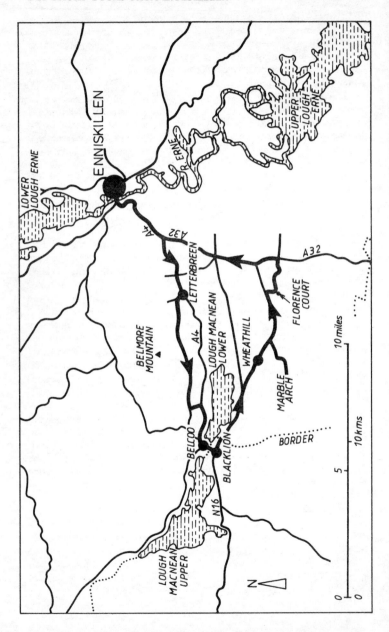

the effort is well repaid by a quiet and scenic road delightful to cycle. Go straight through a crossroads after 5 miles and after a further 1.5 miles rejoin the main B52 road. Go right (west) half a mile and then right (north) for Derrygonnelly. This road rises slowly through lonely but lovely countryside to eventually drop down under the towering cliffs of Knockmore to a right turn (after 7.4 miles) for Boho (don't be tempted to go to Derrygonnelly as this leaves you on a very boring road back to Enniskillen). Continue in the direction of Boho 6.2 miles to a crossroads. Go through this crossroads and follow on to a bridge after 3.2 miles. Cross the bridge and immediately go right for a mile to join the main B81 Derrygonnelly–Enniskillen road and a pleasant downhill cycle back to Enniskillen. Total mileage approx. 42 miles/67 km.

4. Circuit of Belmore Mountain

A short but hilly and very interesting cycle with fine views, particularly in its central section.

Follow Route 3 to Belcoo. From there go north for Boho via the gap between Belmore Mountain and Aghanaglack, rising approx. 400 feet in a short distance to a pass from which it is a very pleasant downhill cycle to the crossroads near Boho described in Route 3 and from there back to Enniskillen. Total mileage 27 miles/43 km.

5. Marble Arch and Florence Court

This is a short route but has the advantage of affording the opportunity to visit Marble Arch Cave and beautiful Florence Court.

Take the route already described to Belcoo and cross the Border to Blacklion. From Blacklion go east along the south shore of Lough Macnean Lower, re-crossing the Border almost immediately. At 5 miles turn right and follow the signposts for Marble Arch (Commercial Cave) which is well worth a visit. After this cave, which is about two miles off the route described and is reached after a climb of a few hundred feet, continue on the same road (east) and visit Florence Court, which has a long and distinguished history. From here, it is 6 miles to Enniskillen. Total mileage for the day (including Marble Arch and Florence Court diversions) approx. 32 miles/51 km.

6. Circuit of Lower Lough Erne

See diversion from Grand Tour day 27.

✓ Apart from a few good pubs in and around the centre of Enniskillen, there is Franco's pub and restaurant also fairly central. This excellent pub/restaurant serves good, reasonably priced food with occasional music and is well recommended.

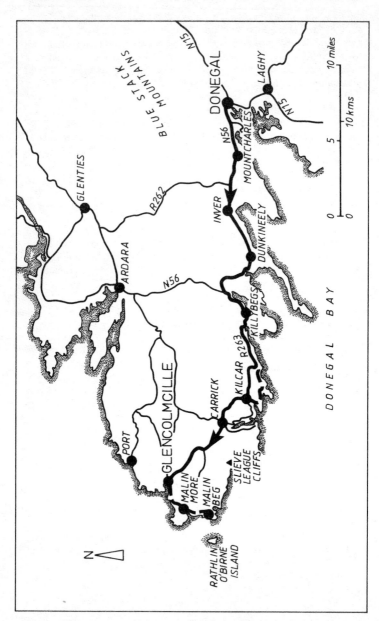

Donegal via Killybegs to Glencolmcille ★★

33 miles/53 km

Description of route: a busy road as far as Killybegs and from there a lovely undulating road to Glencolmcille giving numerous opportunities for detours. It would be ★★★★ save for the traffic as far as Killybegs. A short day which allows some time to be spent in Malin More and Malin Beg, a few miles beyond Glencolmcille.

From Donegal town take the N56 west following the signposts for Killybegs. 1 mile west of Donegal town is a road leading left (south) 1 mile to Ball Hill IYHA Hostel. The road is undulating and busy. Mountcharles, a hilly village associated with Lord Mountcharles of Slane, County Meath, is reached after 4 miles and 2 miles further is the right turn R262/L74 which leads to Glenties and Dungloe which, from this point, are 13 and 30 miles away respectively. Continue on the N56 through Inver and Dunkineely and Bruckless (IH hostel) a further 12 miles to Killybegs, an interesting small town and a major fishing port which will well repay some time spent there. It was granted borough status in 1616 by King James and has extensive links with Scotland, particularly the Hebrides. From Killybegs the R263/T72a continues west along the coast of Donegal Bay with fine views south on a clear day to Benbulben and the mountains of Sligo and Mayo. After 3.5 miles the road goes inland over a 450-ft pass, but this can be avoided by sticking with the lesser graded road by the sea to rejoin the main road to Kilcar (IH hostel). 3 miles after Kilcar is Carrick, at which point one is entering a Gaeltacht (Irish-speaking) area. Continue on over high hills at the back of Slieve League to Glencolmcille, where accommodation can be obtained.

Recommended lunch stop
Killybegs.

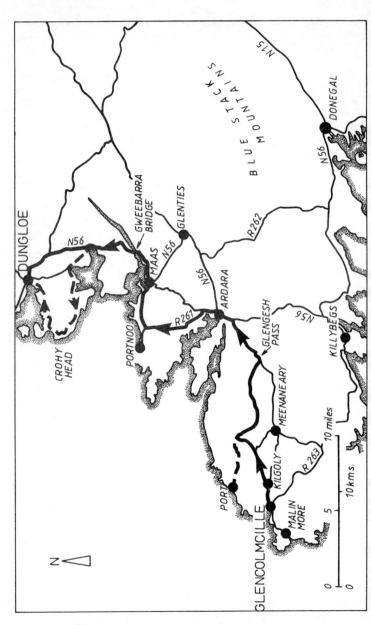

Glencolmcille to Dungloe

42 miles/67 km (including diversion to Port)

Description of route: a hilly but rewarding day with plenty of variety and splendid scenery on offer.

From Cashel in Glencolmcille take the road east 1.5 miles to Kilgoly, then turn left and follow this road for almost 4 miles until a minor road is reached running east–west. This minor road going west leads to the small harbour of Port which is 4 miles away but is well worth a visit. From Port return as you have come but do not turn south for Kilgoly. Instead continue east until you join the main Carrick–Ardara road just before it reaches the top of the Glengesh Pass. Cross the very scenic Glengesh Pass and continue to Ardara. 1 mile after Ardara the road to Maas goes right but a more enjoyable route is to continue on the R261/L81 north and then east around the coast (passing close by Portnoo Golf Club) to Maas and from there over Gweebarra Bridge and on to Dungloe (IH hostel).

If time permits go left 3 miles after Gweebarra Bridge and follow the coast around by Crohy Head (IYHA hostel) adding about 6 miles to your journey but being rewarded with superb views. This is the reverse of Route One in the following ½ day Routes from Dungloe.

Recommended lunch stop
Port or the Glengesh Pass.

✓ *En route* are the Nesbitt Arms in Ardara, the Narin in Narin/Portnoo, and Hylands Hotel in Glenties (if detouring that way). In Dungloe, Sweeneys Hotel is reasonably priced, middle-of-the-distance plain-good-food and centrally located. The Bayview Bar (which doesn't have a view of the bay!) is a well recommended pub.

Note that it is possible to cut out Glencolmcille by taking the road west from Donegal town to the R262/L74 already described and from there north through Maas (after Maas on the N56) to Dungloe in one day.

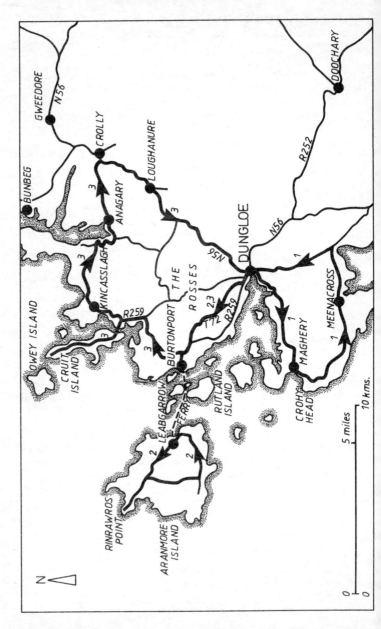

Three ½-day Routes from Dungloe

Route One
Approx. 10 miles/16 km plus detours

Take the road on the south shore to Maghery. From where it rises steeply around Crohy Head past the IYHA hostel, there are superb views from the highest point. The road follows around the headland, undulating until it drops down to Meenacross, from which return north to Dungloe. This route can be incorporated into Grand Tour day 29 if making good time.

Route Two
Approx. 16 miles/26 km plus detours

From Dungloe take the road north west to Burtonpoint (which was once the train terminus of a rail line that ran from Letterkenny) from where, on a continual basis, a RO-RO ferry operates via a passage between Rutland Island and Inishcoo to Aranmore, where there is Leabgarrow IYHA hostel. From Leabgarrow Pier where you disembark from the ferry it is approx. 3 miles past Loch Shore to the Lighthouse at Rinrawros Point on the north-west point of the island along a rough but passable road. When returning from the lighthouse it is possible to cut across the hills directly south on bad but passable, though rough, unmarked tracks to drop down to the south shore of the island. To the south is Inishkeeragh (now uninhabited), where Peadar O'Donnell, author of *Islanders*, was once a school teacher. The road continues around Leabgarrow from where you return to Burtonport.

✓ The Lobster Pot Bar on the pier at Burtonport does some pub grub.

Route Three
Approx. 16 miles/26 km plus 3 miles/5 km each way to end of Cruit Island

From Dungloe go for Burtonport on the T72, after which follow the road around to Kincasslagh, but if time permits along the way go to the end of Cruit Island which is reached by a causeway. After Kincasslagh and Mullaghderg is Annagry, with its myriad of sandy beaches (though take care, as some of them are dangerous for swimming). After Annagry take the road for Loughanure and from there return to Dungloe.

✓ In Kincasslagh a little after the turn-off for Cruit Island is Iggy's Bar which makes a worthwhile stop.

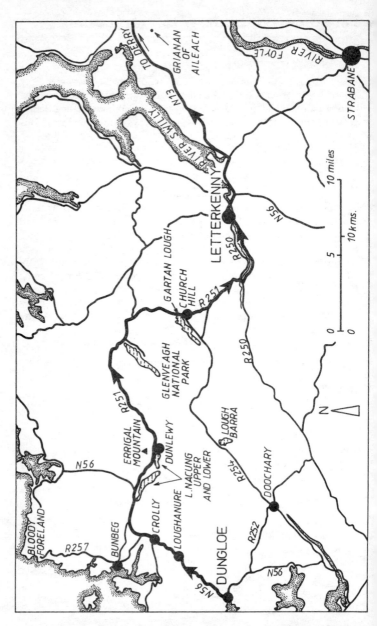

Dungloe via Dunlewy to Letterkenny and Derry ★★★

41 miles/66 km, plus 22 miles/35 km to Derry

Description of route: a fairly tough day with a rise of 850 feet from sea level; through some beautiful country with superb mixed vistas of mountains, lakes and sea.

Leave Dungloe by the N56 going north east to Loughanure and Crolly. About a mile after Crolly the main road goes left for Bunbeg and Bloody Foreland. A further mile on is a bridge with a T junction at Gweedore village (on the left is a ruined railway bridge). Go right (east) along the shores of Lough Nacung Lower. After the ugly power station fork right towards Dunlewy (IYHA hostel) along the shores of Lough Nacung Upper and under the slopes of the beautiful Errigal Mountain. The road — now the R251/L82 — rises around the shoulder of Errigal Mountain, and from near the shoulder the mountain itself can be climbed. (Take care! The top is particularly exposed and can be dangerous in windy conditions.) Continue on the road which drops steeply away from Errigal and turns right (south east), where there is the entrance to Glenveagh National Park. This national park and castle are well worth a visit. From Glenveagh there is a variety of routes back to Letterkenny. It is best to go the quieter road which is via Church Hill. Going this route the last 5 miles into Letterkenny on the R250/L74, which is a busy main road, can be avoided by going right as soon as the R250/L74 is reached and almost immediately left, to follow a third-class road on the south side of the river right into Letterkenny (IH hostel).

Recommended lunch stop
Glenveagh National Park.

✓ There is an Interpretative Centre complete with cafe at Dunlewy which is situated right underneath magnificent Errigal Mountain.

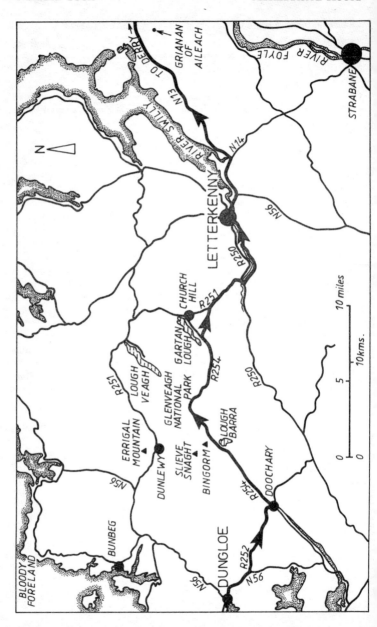

Dungloe via Doochary to Letterkenny and Derry ★★★

33 miles/53 km, plus 22 miles/35 km to Derry

Description of route: a short but mixed and very enjoyable day rising to 700 feet through beautiful country on very quiet roads — at least in its middle section.

Route

From Dungloe go 2.5 miles south east on the N56 then fork left for Doochary on the R252/L75 which is reached after 5 miles. At Doochary turn left on the R254, passing lovely Lough Barra on the right after 5 miles. A further mile on are the cliffs of Bingorm (a favourite with rock climbers), after which the road rises for a further 2.5 miles to a point where there are good views to the north east down into Glenveagh. After crossing the pass the road drops down until, at a point opposite the end of Gartan Lough, there is a right turn. Take this right turn and 2 miles further the R251/L82 is joined, and this is followed quite easily to Letterkenny (IH hostel); though note the quiet back road for the last 5 miles into Letterkenny described at the end of Grand Tour day 30.

Recommended lunch stop

At the top of the pass looking down into Glenveagh National Park.

Note that the road from Letterkenny to Derry has virtually nothing to recommend it, except the Grianan of Aileach, a stone fort a few miles to the south of the road 6 miles west of Derry city. You might consider staying in Letterkenny overnight and doing the approx. 20 miles to Derry early the following morning to catch a train for Coleraine, thereby breaking the day nicely. Because of the Troubles, Northern Ireland did not develop its tourist industry at the same rate as the Republic. Accordingly accommodation is sparse and difficult to locate though the TIOs are very helpful and the tourist industry is quickly catching up. There is a YHANI hostel in Derry City. There are many excellent small restaurants and particularly pubs inside the walled city.

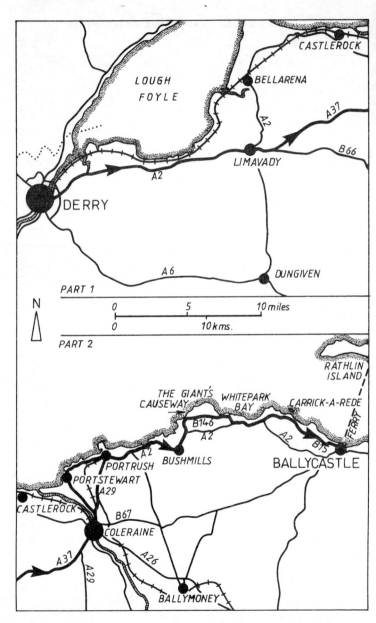

PART 1

N

| 0 | 5 | 10 miles |
| 0 | | 10 kms. |

PART 2

Derry via Coleraine to Ballycastle   ★★★

Various

Description of route: a long day, flat and boring at the start but with The Giant's Causeway and Carrick-a-Rede in the latter half before arriving at Ballycastle. Due to the beauty and reputation of The Giant's Causeway and Carrick-a-Rede it is advisable to use a train from Derry to Coleraine. During the summer there are six or seven trains per day connecting Derry with Coleraine. Those wanting to spend more time at The Giant's Causeway and/or Carrick-a-Rede can connect at Coleraine for Portrush, thereby shortening the cycling part of the day to approx. 20 miles/32 km.

From Derry take the busy A2 17 miles to Limavady. This road has some fine views but otherwise it is a fast busy main road. After Limavady take the A37 a further 13 miles through pleasant country but on a busy road to Coleraine. From Coleraine you can go round the coast via Portstewart (IH hostel) to Portrush or directly to Portrush (8 and 5 miles respectively). Both Portstewart and Portrush are successful resort towns with all the usual facilities. Approx. 3 miles after Portrush is historic and breathtaking Dunluce Castle, the home of the MacDonalds, which should not be missed. From Portrush follow the A2 east 5.5 miles to Bushmills and after Bushmills until signposts are reached for The Giant's Causeway, which should not on any account be missed. The Giant's Causeway is worth at least an hour or two of exploration. From The Giant's Causeway return to the coast road and head east again past Whitepark Bay (YHANI hostel) following signs for Carrick-a-Rede, where a rope bridge 80 feet over the sea connects a rocky islet with the mainland 60 feet away. Though slightly less spectacular than The Giant's Causeway, Carrick-a-Rede should not be missed. Continue after Carrick-a-Rede on the coast road to Ballycastle (IH hostel), which has all the usual facilities and from where a boat can be got if you wish to visit Rathlin Island, which has accommodation and is reputedly the scene of the cave where exiled Scot Robert Bruce learned a lesson in perseverance when he saw the spider try, try and try again.

For those who are into making this a day of sightseeing then at Bushmills, shortly before The Giant's Causeway, is a whiskey distillery which manufactures the famous Bushmills brand and which is open to the public for tours. It is reputed to be the oldest legal distillery in the world, having been granted a licence in 1608.

Recommended lunch stop
The Giant's Causeway.

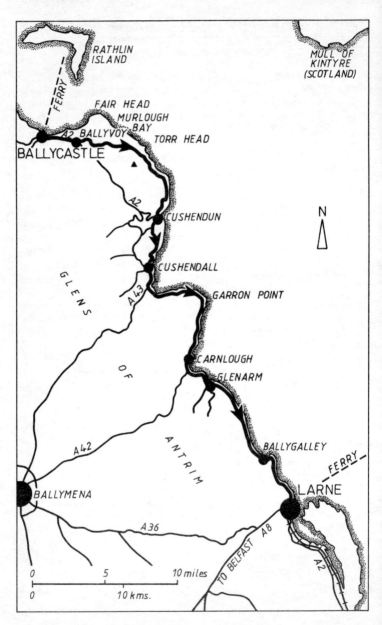

Ballycastle via Larne to Belfast ★★★

41 miles/66 km, plus 20 miles/32 km to Belfast

Description of route: a beautiful route with fine views to Scotland and the Isle of Man, first over Carnamore and Cross Slieve Mountains and then by the side of the sea almost the whole way to Larne and Belfast. The last lap of this route from Larne into Belfast should be done by train which runs quite frequently: more than one per hour. Note, however, that there are two stations in Larne: one in Larne town and the other a little further out at Larne Harbour and not all of the trains go as far as Larne Harbour.

From Ballycastle take the A2 road to the east to Ballyvoy 3.5 miles. At the junction go left and rise to a height of 850 feet as the road crosses the high pass near Torr Head. An excursion (1 mile each way but 600 feet down and up) to Murlough Bay from a junction 2 miles after Ballyvoy would reward the fit cyclist or the top-class rock climber (Fair Head being probably Ireland's toughest rock-climbing area). From the highest point note the Mull of Kintyre to the north east and Rathlin Island behind you to the north west. The road drops mainly down — occasionally up — before arriving at Cushendun. After Cushendun the road by the coast rises over Cross Slieve before dropping down to Cushendall (YHANI hostel). This stretch can be avoided by using the main road A2 to Cushendall but at the expense of wonderful views afforded by the coast road. After Cushendall continue through Carnlough, Glenarm and Ballygalley (YHANI hostel) to Larne.

The distance from Ballycastle by the route described to Larne is 41 miles without detouring for Murlough Bay. Those wanting to cycle to Belfast (YHANI and IH hostels) from Larne will find the most direct route by the A8 a further 20 miles but may have difficulties with motorways at the end, since it is not permitted to cycle on them.

Belfast York Road Station which used to serve only the Larne line is now linked up with Belfast Central Station, which is the main Belfast terminal. If connecting for Dublin then enquire of Northern Ireland Railways.

Recommended lunch stop
Cushendall or Carnlough.

✓ The Londonderry Arms, Carnlough, is a fine old coaching inn doing pub grub.

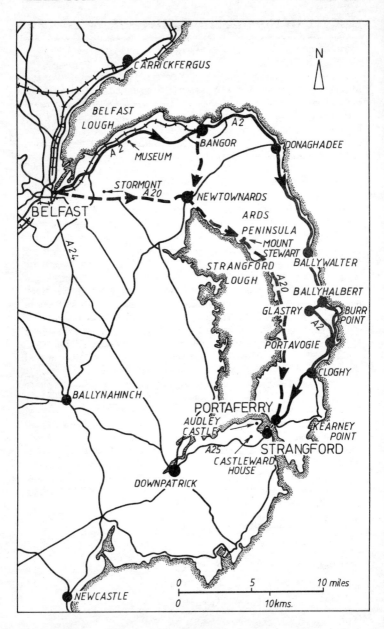

N

CARRICKFERGUS

BELFAST
LOUGH

A2

BANGOR

A2

DONAGHADEE

MUSEUM

STORMONT

A20

BELFAST

NEWTOWNARDS

ARDS

PENINSULA

MOUNT
STEWART

A24

STRANGFORD

LOUGH

BALLYWALTER

A20

BALLYHALBERT

GLASTRY

BURR
POINT

A2

PORTAVOGIE

BALLYNAHINCH

CLOGHY

PORTAFERRY

AUDLEY
CASTLE

KEARNEY
POINT

A25

STRANGFORD

CASTLEWARD
HOUSE

DOWNPATRICK

NEWCASTLE

0   5   10 miles

0   10kms.

Belfast to Portaferry or Strangford ★★

40 miles/64 km

Description of route: a flat but interesting day, heavy with traffic for the first one-third until Bangor and thereafter on a pleasant seaside road down the extreme east coast of Ireland to overnight at Portaferry at the mouth of famous Strangford Lough.

From Belfast take the A2 by the south shore of Belfast Lough past Belfast Harbour Airport for Bangor, which started life as a seaside resort and is now a dormitory town. About halfway along this stretch is the Ulster Folk and Transport Museum which is well worth a visit. Not far away is the imposing edifice of Stormont, former seat of the prorogued Northern Ireland Parliament. For those wishing to avoid traffic it is possible to take the train to Bangor, thereby saving 13 miles, and commence from there. From Bangor keep to the coast road (still A2) to Donaghadee: and 'it's 6 miles from Bangor to Donaghadee', to quote the words of the famous song. From Donaghadee continue down the coast by Ballywalter, following the A2. At Ballyhalbert, which is shortly before Glastry, the A2 road goes inland via Glastry but there is a road by the shore which should be taken, if only because it goes to Burr Point, the most easterly part of Ireland. Whichever road you take, continue on to Portavogie and from there to Cloghy, from where the road goes inland to Portaferry. At Cloghy it is possible to take a left turn for Kearney Point, which is a worthwhile detour and from where it is a straight run across the neck of the Ards Peninsula to Portaferry (YHANI hostel). One can overnight at Portaferry or at Strangford on the opposite side; the ferry runs continuously all day long.

A shorter cycle is to take the A20 from Newtownards down the inside of the peninsula, passing Mount Stewart, a National Trust property famous for its gardens and its history — it was the home of Lord Castlereagh, the chief negotiator for the British at the Conference of Vienna in 1815.

Of interest, on the north side of the A25 road west from Strangford, is Castle Ward. A little to the north is Audley Castle which is also worth a visit. Indeed, this part of Ireland is littered with castles and churches.

Recommended lunch stop
Donaghadee or Mount Stewart.

✓ The Portaferry Inn has long been an example of a well-run hotel in a beautiful setting. It has a deserved reputation for good food.

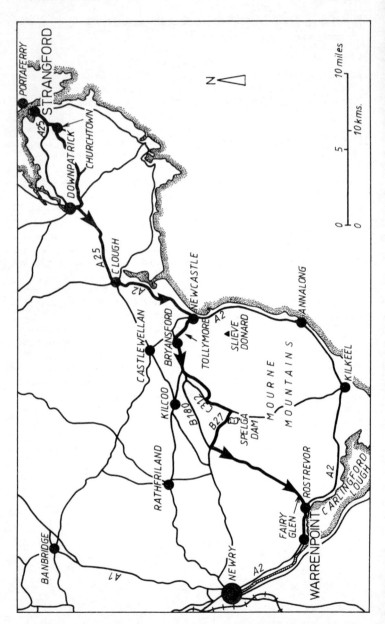

Strangford to Warrenpoint   ★★

38 miles/61 km

Description of route: an interesting and varied route first on the East Down lowlands then through the Mourne Mountains to Carlingford Lough and Newry, from where there are a number of trains each day to Belfast and to Dublin. As far as Newcastle the route merits only ★ because of traffic but thereafter would merit ★★★ so ★★ is a compromise between the two parts.

From Strangford on the west side of the channel take the A25 1.5 miles to a left turn signposted for Churchtown. Go a short distance on this road to a church on the left after which there is a right turn for Downpatrick. Downpatrick itself is an ancient seat of learning and its cathedral, which is the burial place of Saint Patrick, deserves a visit, as does the Down County Museum (once a jail) which is adjacent. After Downpatrick the A25 road is fairly level for 6 miles to Clough at which you should take the A2 for 6 miles to Newcastle (YHANI hostel).

From Newcastle take the B180 to the entrance to Tollymore Forest Park. Go through the park and at the exit turn left, still on the B180. This road goes across the northern edge of the Mourne Mountains with fine views of the famous range and Slieve Donard, the highest point at 2,788 feet. Just over 1.5 miles from the exit gate from Tollymore and just after a right-hand fork for Kilcoo and Rathfriland there is a minor road to the left. Take this very pleasant and quiet road which first drops down to the river and then gently rises until it reaches a T junction on the C312. Go left and continue for 2 miles until the Spelga Dam is visible on the right, at which point the road is at a height of 1,300 feet. Go right on the B27 passing the Spelga Dam on the left and dropping down until 2 miles after the Spelga Dam, and having dropped 900 feet in altitude, a crossroads is reached. Go left at this crossroads and up a pleasant wooded valley rising gently to a height of 675 feet in 3.5 miles before dropping down 4 miles to Rostrevor through a delightful wooded glen alongside the Ulster Way on the left with many picnic sites. The last 7 miles would be the high point of the day. From Rostrevor it is 2 miles to Warrenpoint. If going to Newry for the train note that the station is on the west side of the town; enquire locally.

Recommended lunch stop
Tollymore Forest Park.

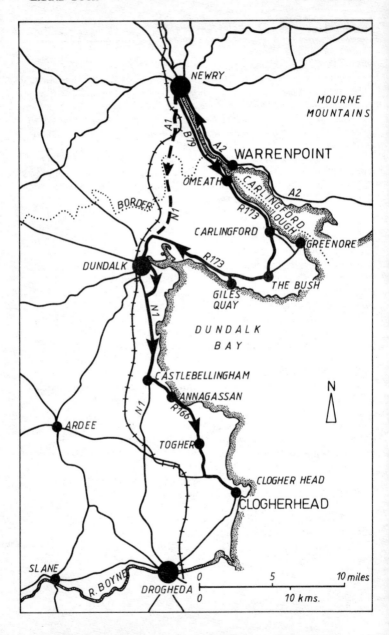

Warrenpoint to Clogherhead ★★

52 miles/83 km via Newry

Description of route: a long but fairly flat and very varied route starting in Northern Ireland, taking in Newry and the Cooley Peninsula, through Dundalk to Clogherhead, a pleasant seaside resort north of Drogheda.

From Warrenpoint take the A2 7 miles into Newry on an unpleasantly fast and busy but scenic road. At Newry either take the main Dublin road (A1) to the Border and then the N1 to Dundalk or (preferably) follow the road down the west side of the river/lough, first on the B79 (Northern Ireland designation) and then — after the Border — the R173/T62 through Omeath (IYHA hostel) to Carlingford (IH hostel). Carlingford itself is a beautiful village steeped in history, and deserves at least a little time of exploration and enjoyment. The road then continues around to the south of the peninsula. An optional excursion off the road to the south 5 miles after Carlingford is Giles Quay. Continue on the R173/T62 to join the main Dublin–Belfast (N1) road 2 miles north of Dundalk. During the summer it is possible to cross from Warrenpoint to Omeath by ferry with bikes; and as this gives time to explore the Cooley Peninsula and cuts out the Warrenpoint–Newry road, it is recommended. For details enquire locally or phone Warrenpoint Tourist Information Office.

As you come into Dundalk cross the bridge and to avoid the town follow the signs for Dublin so that you exit onto the N1 again 2 miles south of Dundalk. Continue south on this busy road 6 miles to Castlebellingham, at which turn left and follow the R166/L6 through Annagassan and Togher to Clogherhead.

Recommended lunch stop
Carlingford or Giles Quay.

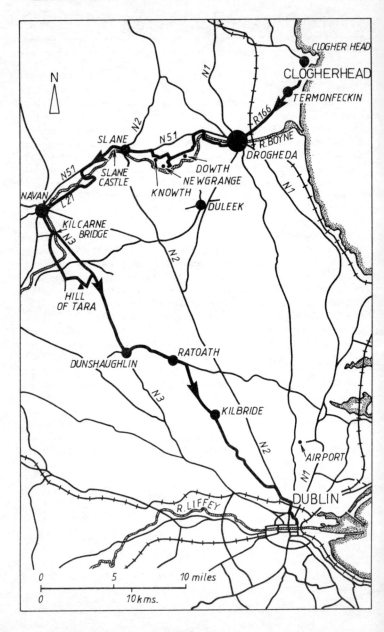

Clogherhead via Boyne Valley and
Tara to Dublin   ★★★

55 miles/88 km

Description of route: a long and flat day taking in historic Newgrange and Knowth, continuing to the Hill of Tara and from there down a reasonably quiet road to the city of Dublin.

From Clogherhead take the R166/L6 through Termonfeckin 8 miles to Drogheda.

(Note that as navigation is a little tricky in this area distances are given accurate to one-tenth of a mile.)

Leave Drogheda by the main Dublin (N1) road and go right (west) just to the south side of the river. From where this road leaves the main Dublin–Belfast road go for 1.2 miles to a fork/T junction, at which go right to join the river. This is a bad road not shown on the Michelin map. A further 1.3 miles brings you to the canal navigation section and a further 0.1 miles to a bridge across the river. It is just to the west of this bridge that on 1 July 1690 took place the Battle of the Boyne, which decided the fate of Ireland, the British throne and the balance of power in Europe. Having crossed the River Boyne go west on the main Drogheda–Slane road (N51) for 0.9 miles and then follow the signposts for prehistoric Dowth, Newgrange and Knowth. The best known of these is Newgrange. Dowth is closed for exploration and rebuilding. Knowth was opened to the public in July 1991. From Dowth follow the signposts for Newgrange, which will be found 3.5 miles after leaving the main road. From there follow the signposts for Knowth, after which comes the first major choice of route. If Newgrange/Dowth/Knowth has taken most of the day then you could return to Drogheda for an evening train, of which there are a number. Alternatively, you could continue to Slane, passing on the way the home of Francis Ledwidge, the well-known Irish poet who was born in Slane in 1887 and killed in Belgium in 1917. The cottage is open during the summer season as a small memorial to the poet. From Slane go west on the N51, passing by Slane Castle on the left between you and the river. It was severely damaged by fire in late 1991. At 4.5 miles after Slane turn left at a junction signposted for Ardmulchan. After half a mile cross the River Boyne immediately and go left up a little wooded glen and under a disused railway line to a T junction. Go right on to the L21 signposted 4 miles for Navan. 2.4 miles after crossing the bridge there is a small detour well worth taking: go 300 yards right (north) to a viewing point at a graveyard high above the river with Dunmoe Castle in view. Return to the main road and proceed to Navan. From where this road crosses the river at the outskirts of Navan turn left and proceed along the Dublin road (N3) 3.9 miles to a right turn up to the Hill of Tara, which is reached after a further 0.8 miles.

For the more adventurous who would prefer to avoid the grind of the main road from Navan south to Dublin, a more rewarding route is as follows. Take the Dublin road 1 mile from Navan to a right turn just after the old Kilcarne Bridge and just before the new bridge. The road is signposted Cannistown 1 mile. After half a mile the Cannistown road goes right but you proceed straight for Tara along a road not marked on the Michelin map. After a further 1.5 miles the river is crossed again and after a further half mile the road crosses a main road. Proceed across the intersection and from there 0.8 miles to a left turn directly opposite the unmistakable gates of Royal Tara Golf Club. Follow on 0.4 miles to a right turn with a missing signpost and then up the hill over a bad road 1 mile to the car park fronting the Hill of Tara.

From Tara drop down east to the main Dublin–Navan (N3) road. Go approx. 4 miles to Dunshaughlin and from there turn left for Ratoath, from where there is a relatively traffic-free road back through Kilbride into the city centre.

Recommended lunch stop
Hill of Tara.

OTHER ROUTES

Boyne Valley

The following two tours are routes that can easily be done in a day. There is a very great difference between them. The Boyne Valley route is a low-level, fairly flat tour which concentrates on Ireland's ancient history and includes Newgrange, which is now accepted as being the oldest known 'building' in Europe, whereas the Rathdrum route takes in the beautiful Vale of Clara, Glendalough with its monastic history and the Wicklow Mountains, and is a little hilly. Because Dublin is a capital city with almost a million people it is best if possible to avoid unnecessary struggles with traffic, so on both routes there is an option to return by train. When purchasing your ticket you should enquire the price of a return ticket even if not intending to take it, because very often a return ticket can be acquired for the same price as a single ticket, thereby keeping options open. The second route largely retraces Grand Tour day 1 and part of day 2.

Boyne Valley

From Dublin (Connolly Station/Amiens Street) take the early-morning train for Drogheda. The journey takes approx. 35 minutes.

From Drogheda follow the description given in Grand Tour day 36.

From Tara to return to Dublin either:
1. Follow the directions for Dunshaughlin and Ratoath given in Grand Tour day 36 and from there into the city centre; or
2. Drop down 0.8 miles east to the main Dublin–Navan (N3/T35) road and turn left for Navan. Go 1.1 miles to a crossroads signposted for Bective Abbey at Taranaree public house. Go right (east) for Duleek and follow signposts with no great difficulty through double T junctions, crossing the main Dublin–Slane road (N2) after 5.9 miles and a further 4.1 miles to Duleek, and thence to Drogheda, returning by train.

Finally it would be as well to read some brochures about the Boyne Valley and the Hill of Tara before taking this route. In the National Gallery there is an excellent little map and guide, *Antiquities of the Boyne Valley*, on sale very cheaply but the area would, of course, repay more detailed study as there are many more castles, abbeys, fortifications and prehistoric sites in the area than have been referred to in this chapter.

Rathdrum via Glendalough to Dublin

Take the morning train from Connolly Station/Amiens Street to Rathdrum, 70 minutes approx. A fit cyclist could during early summer (for reasons of light) manage the entire trip (provided not too much time was spent in Glendalough) by departing on the lunchtime train. From Rathdrum cycle up the west side of the beautiful Vale of Clara to Laragh on the R755/T61. This is a magnificent stretch of quiet road through a beautiful wooded glen 7 miles to Laragh and a further 1.5 miles to Glendalough.

From Glendalough take the road back to Laragh and having crossed the bridge turn left, following the signpost for Sally Gap. The road from here back into the suburbs of Dublin was built by the British to quell the rebellious Irish and is known as the Military Road. The road rises gradually through Glenmacnass and then steeply at the head of the glen to above the Glenmacnass Waterfall which is visible for some miles. At the top of the waterfall there are some pools beside the road which make wonderful swimming pools! However, care must be taken near the waterfall as there have been several serious (including fatal) accidents at this point. From the head of the waterfall continue on through spectacular open country to Sally Gap, which is merely a crossroads in the mountains, and from there a further 2 miles on what is now the R115/L94, at which point you cross a small stream at a place called Liffey Head Bridge. This is the stream which becomes the River Liffey which flows through the centre of Dublin. Shortly after Liffey Head Bridge the road drops sharply down into the head of Glencree Valley where (2.5 miles after Liffey Head Bridge) one is given a choice of route. After a steep descent and a few hundred yards after a little cottage on the left there is a road swinging back to the right and down. If you wish you can take this road (which requires hardly any pedalling for 5 miles) to the gate of Powerscourt Demesne leading into Powerscourt Waterfall which is well worth a visit. After Powerscourt there is a short steep uphill section, after which go through a crossroads and then drop down to join a T junction; go straight and keep left at the next fork to the Rocky Valley. From the Rocky Valley drop down on the R755/T61 to Kilmacanoge, after which you go left on the main Dublin road (N11) and follow the signposts to Bray and its railway station which will bring you back to Connolly Station/Amiens Street.

If not wishing to take the route via Powerscourt Demesne through to Bray then continue across the top of the Glencree Valley to a fork. Go left leaving the old Reformatory on the right and follow the signposts for Rathfarnham. This will bring you over another stage of the mountains and on to Killakee car park. Follow the signposts from there to Rathfarnham and thence to the city centre.

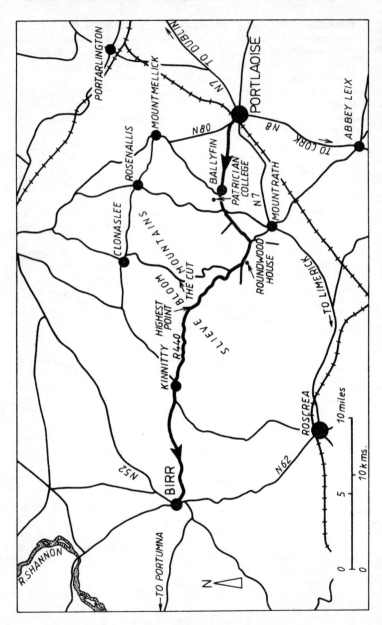

Dublin/Portlaoise to Birr ★★★

31 miles/49 km

Description of route: a well worthwhile way of getting out of Dublin and on the way to the west of Ireland to join the Grand Tour. Day 1 of this route is shorter than the average route in this book on a mileage basis but does cross the Slieve Bloom Mountains. The route ends up in Birr which is a small town with much political, architectural, botanical and astronomical history, and is well worth a few hours on its own.

There are numerous trains each day from Heuston Station to Portlaoise, a journey of about an hour.

In order to follow this route it is important to follow the instructions below very carefully or else to pick one's route over the mountains with the aid of OS sheet 15 half-inch scale or the newer 1:50,000 map of the Slieve Blooms also published by Ordnance Survey. The Michelin map is unhelpful in this area in a number of respects.

Leaving the railway station at Portlaoise go west along the line of the railway track for 200 yards to a T junction. Go right under the railway bridge and continue until just after a Dunnes Stores supermarket on the right there is a left fork signposted 5.5 miles Ballyfin. After 5.5 miles a T junction is reached, facing a large estate wall. Go left, keeping the estate wall on the right. After a further 1 mile a main gate into the estate — a Patrician College — is reached on the right. A few hundred yards after the college entrance there is a right turn signposted for Rosenallis which is to be ignored. A few hundred yards further is an unsignposted right turn off the main road. Take this road. Ignore an unsignposted right turn 1.2 miles further on and continue a further 2 miles along the road to a T junction, at which go right. This road is signposted for Mountain Drive and Roundwood House (a magnificent Palladian mansion — now an acclaimed guest house), shortly after which there is a shop on the right followed by a right turn signposted for Kinnitty. Take this road. After 2.4 miles cross a bridge and at a fork immediately afterwards go left up a hill signposted for Kinnitty. From here the road rises continuously for almost 4 miles to the top of the Slieve Bloom range. It is said that on a clear day from here the highest points in all four provinces of Ireland can be seen. It is believed that somewhere in this immediate locality the last wolf in Ireland was killed.

About a mile beyond the top of the road there is a fork, at which go left as signposted to Kinnitty. After Kinnitty the road is relatively flat and signposted for Birr for the remaining 7.5 miles.

Recommended lunch stop
Either the highest point of the Slieve Bloom Mountains or Kinnitty.

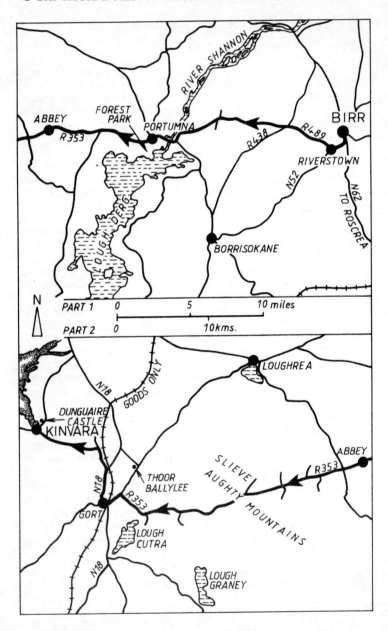

Birr via Gort to Kinvara   ★

52 miles/83 km

Description of route: a mundane but quiet and enjoyable route with a number of interesting interludes. Some boring stretches but some interesting aspects. If going from Portlaoise to North Clare it probably cannot be avoided so best make the most of it!

From Birr take the main south road (N62) signposted for Roscrea and Portumna and almost immediately fork right for Riverstown. At Riverstown (after less than a mile) go right on the R489/T41 signposted for Portumna across the River Brosna.

After a further 4.5 miles cross the R438/L113 to reach a fork; go right, signposted for Portumna. Continue to Portumna crossing the River Shannon about 1 mile before Portumna. Between the River Shannon and Portumna is a harbour very popular with holiday cruisers; it is worth a short visit. Then take the left fork as you enter the town and go through the gate of the forest park to the marina. If desired, take one of the various forest walks with fine views of Lough Derg and Portumna Castle (under restoration). When you leave through the forest gates turn left and rejoin the main road, turning left again on to it and following the signs for Gort. After almost 8 miles is the tiny but interesting village of Abbey. 1.6 miles after Abbey a T junction is reached; go right signposted for Gort and turn left immediately, signposted for Gort. The road (R353/L55) goes through some quite enjoyable open country rising to a height of 550 feet before dropping to a junction signposted 1 mile for Gort; total distance Portumna to Gort 28 miles.

After Gort leave by the Galway road (N18) and after 2.4 miles take a left turn, signposted for Kinvara. Go a further 2.3 miles to a crossroads at which go left, signposted for Kinvara. After a short distance notice a memorial on the right-hand side to Padraig and Henry O'Lactan who died at that spot in November 1920 in a fight with the British Forces of occupation.

A little further on beautiful Kinvara with its magnificent Dunguaire Castle and other facilities, including nearby Doorus House (Burren IYHA hostel) 4 miles from Kinvara, is reached.

Recommended lunch stop
Portumna or Abbey.

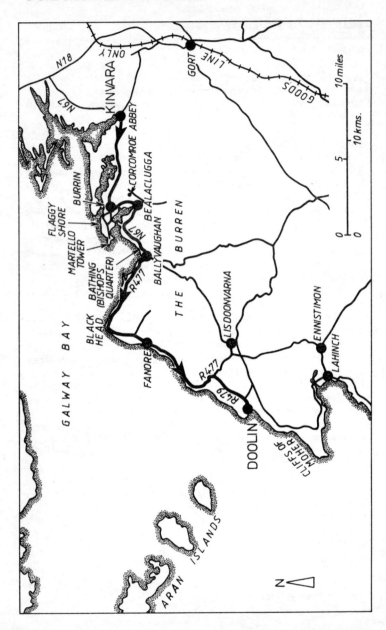

Kinvara to Doolin   ★★★

35 miles/56 km plus detours

Description of route: a magnificent day following the coast around to Doolin with superb views, castles and abbeys, good pubs, no serious altitude, to arrive at Doolin with its traditional hospitality.

Follow the road west from Kinvara into the Burren. After 6.5 miles there is a right turn at Burrin for Finnavarra. This is an interesting excursion on a little-visited peninsula to a Martello Tower (one of a series built around 200 years ago to resist the French). After going to the end of the peninsula one can return by Lough Morree and the Flaggy Shore back to Burrin village; perhaps 5.5 miles. After Burrin proceed along the main road south to Bealaclugga (Bell Harbour). At Bealaclugga a short detour is recommended: go left (south) to Daly's public house on the left and about 50/60 yards after the public house turn left up bad road to Corcomroe Abbey. Although this road is rutted and difficult to navigate it well repays the effort.

Returning to the road continue around the coast for nearly a mile to a turn for a ruined castle on the right — worth a visit.

Approx. 2.5 miles further west on the right is a beach, and if the tide is right this is a most pleasant one to visit.

A little further on is Ballyvaughan where the traveller can rest. This can be done in the village itself or at Monk's public house a little to the west of the village (recommended). Ballyvaughan has a justified reputation for the culinary arts, and some time should be spent there.

After Ballyvaughan the road continues round the south coast of Galway Bay between the limestone drills of North Clare and the Atlantic Ocean. At 1.5 miles after Ballyvaughan, Gleninagh Castle, which was occupied until 1840, is well worth a visit.

Continue round the coast to Black Head and then south to Fanore, just before which on the left is the Caher River, the only overland river in the Burren. A short detour up this pretty glen is worthwhile, then return to the road to Fanore. The beach invites at least a short walk, though swimming is definitely risky and not to be recommended.

Follow the road south to a crossroads 0.7 miles after leaving the sea, at which point go right for Doolin or straight on for Lisdoonvarna, as is one's choice.

Recommended lunch stop
Ballyvaughan.

Cycle-Touring Weekends from Dublin

This chapter is for those who wish to consider two- or three-day weekends (the latter adding a Friday or a Monday to Saturday and Sunday to avail of weekend return train fares) from Dublin. All of them extensively use trains which get to Westport, Killarney, etc. by about midday the first day. Some of the days described are 50 miles/80 km plus. As most of these trips take in parts of the Grand Tour, only short details are given.

2-day Trips

1. Dublin to Westport by train, then R335/T39 to Louisburg, then south via Doolough and Leenane, after which continue to Lough Fee and the coast road (to here reversing Grand Tour day 22) to the Renvyle/Tully Cross area (overnight); returning by Kylemore Abbey and Leenane, then either:

(a) south on R336/L100 4.5 miles then left and over a low pass to Lough Nafooey and along the west side of Lough Mask through Tourmakeady (where the great actor Robert Shaw lived and died), following on to the beautifully restored Ballintober Abbey, then through Cornanagh to Claremorris;

(b) straight back from Leenane to Westport on the main N59 route. This is the shortest and — with the prevailing winds from the south — usually the fastest way home;

(c) from Leenane again south through the Maam Valley on the R336/L100 to Cornamona beside Lough Corrib, then via Clonbur to Cong (location of the epic John Wayne film, *The Quiet Man*), then first via the R345/L101 and then the R334/L98 to Ballinrobe. After Ballinrobe follow the R331/L20 to Hollymount and Claremorris; then, in each case, by train to Dublin.

2. Dublin to Westport by train, then north to Newport and along the shores of Lough Feeagh and by a beautiful third-class road (not on all maps) north to Keenagh, Rake Street, Crossmolina and Ballina (overnight); Lough Talt, Cloonacool and Coolaney (to this point the two days follow the Grand Tour days 25 and 26) to Collooney, returning by train to Dublin.

3. Dublin to Limerick Junction (not Limerick city), changing trains to go on to Carrick-on-Suir then (following Grand Tour day 5) Suir Valley, Clonmel, the Vee, Lismore (overnight); then either:

(a) Fermoy, Mallow (Grand Tour day 6), returning by train to Dublin; or

(b) Dungarvan, Waterford city, returning by train to Dublin.

Cycle-Touring Weekends from Dublin

4. Dublin to Westport by train, then following the Achill route described in Grand Tour day 23, and returning from Westport by train to Dublin.

5. Dublin to Sligo by train, then either by the very scenic N16 through Glencar or by the quieter R286/L16 by the shores of Lough Gill to Manorhamilton and Blacklion to Enniskillen (overnight); then by any of a variety of routes (see section on one-day tours from Enniskillen) to Ballinamore and either to Carrick-on-Shannon or Dromod, returning by train to Dublin.

6. Dublin to Athy by train, then south to Carlow and then by the west side of the River Barrow to Leighlinbridge, after which follow the river's east side to Bagenalstown (equally well known by its Irish name, Muine Bheag), Borris, Graiguenamanagh, Inistioge (overnight); then either:

(a) north to Thomastown, Bennettsbridge, Kilkenny, Ballyragget, then by the R432/T14 to Ballinakill, Abbeyleix and then by the R425/L126 (very necessary to avoid heavy traffic on the Dublin–Cork main road) to Portlaoise, returning by train to Dublin; or

(b) south east to New Ross, north to St Mullins and the east side of the River Barrow, then over the 650-ft scenic Scullogue Gap to Enniscorthy, returning by train to Dublin.

7. Dublin to Ballinasloe by train then south to Portumna and east to Birr (overnight); Kinnitty, the Slieve Blooms (being careful to follow the directions in Day 1 of the 3-day Portlaoise–Doolin route in reverse), Ballyfin, Portlaoise, returning by train to Dublin. If the weather is not suitable for the Slieve Blooms there are alternatives: either go south of the mountains to Ballybrophy or north of the mountains to Portarlington, both of which have trains to Dublin, though more frequently from Portarlington.

8. Dublin to Westport by train, south west to Leenane, then either the coast road by Tully Cross or directly by Kylemore Abbey into Letterfrack, Clifden (overnight); Ballinaboy, east to Toombeola, Cashel, Gortmore, Screeb, Costelloe and Inverin, then suffer a busy road to Galway, returning by train to Dublin. This route can be done more enjoyably in reverse as you could reasonably expect the prevailing winds behind you on the road into Westport.

Cycle-Touring Weekends from Dublin

9. Dublin to Birdhill by train, then west to O'Briensbridge and across a low gap to Broadford, following on to O'Callaghansmills on the R466/L31, Moymore, Fairgreen to Barefield, then across the main Ennis–Galway (N18) road and through Ruan to Corofin, then by Kilfenora to Lisdoonvarna and Doolin (overnight); then via Black Head, Ballyvaughan, Kinvara, Ardrahan, Craughwell and north to Athenry, returning by train to Dublin.

Note that this route has two long days of 50-plus miles each, and careful navigation is required in the middle stages of the first day and at the end of the second day. The first day particularly requires careful navigation which, without OS sheets 18, 14 and (especially) 17, would be very difficult.

3-day Trips

1. Dublin to Killarney by train, then to Cahirciveen (overnight); the Skelligs, Waterville (overnight); Sneem, Killarney, returning by train to Dublin. Note that Waterville is 53 miles from Killarney, so that Caherdaniel or even Sneem might be considered better as an overnight stop.

2. Dublin to Farranfore by train, then west by way of Castlemaine and Inch to Dingle (overnight); Dunquin/the Blaskets, Dingle (overnight again); the Connor Pass, returning by train from Tralee to Dublin. This route has the advantage of allowing your belongings to be left in Dingle during the second day.

3. Dublin to Millstreet by train, then following Grand Tour day 8 south to Glengarriff (overnight); Castletownbere (overnight); visiting Bere Island or, for the very fit, day 9 of the Grand Tour (Dursey Island, Allihies), then back by way of Kenmare to Killarney, returning by train to Dublin.

4. Dublin to Westport by train, then north to Newport, Mulrany, west to Achill (overnight); Mulrany, north to Belmullet (overnight); North Mayo, east to Killala, Ballina, returning by train to Dublin. Note there is only one train on Sundays to Dublin from Ballina, leaving at the rather early time of 15.25.

Cycle-Touring Weekends from Dublin

5. Dublin to Westport by train, then either west via Louisburg and Doolough or directly to Leenane, then either via the coast road to Tully Cross or directly by Kylemore Abbey to the Letterfrack area (overnight); then west to visit Cleggan and Omey Island (if the tide is out) and possibly the Sky Road Peninsula (where Peter O'Toole maintains a house), through Clifden and round the coast through Ballyconneely to Roundstone (overnight); then east to Toombeola, Cashel, Gortmore, Screeb, Costelloe and Inverin after which suffer a busy road to Galway, returning by train to Dublin.

Note that there are many variations to this route. For example, if you overnighted the first night in Clifden you could easily make it to Rossaveal and from there out on to the Aran Islands, returning from there on day three to Galway.

IYHA has a good-value deal providing two nights' hostel accommodation and return rail fare to any train station in the Republic for £23, to which must be added the cost of transportation of your bike (maximum £6 each way) so that for up to a maximum of £35 you get rail transport for passenger and bike and two overnight accommodation vouchers. For further details apply IYHA, 61 Mountjoy Street, Dublin 7, Phone (01) 830 4555, Fax (01) 830 5808.

YHANI has similar packages based on the Antrim coast and Castle Archdale hostel on Lough Erne. For details contact YHANI at 56 Bradbury Place, Belfast, Phone (01232) 324733, Fax (01232) 439699 (first dial 08 if phoning from the Republic).

Useful Telephone Numbers

Dublin Tourism operates a walk-in system only from St Andrew Street Church, St Andrew Street, Dublin, although there is an information line on 1550 112233. However, for those outside the Republic of Ireland, Dublin Tourism is available at Phone: Dublin (01) 605 7797, Fax: Dublin (01) 605 7787. Other tourist-orientated organisations are more helpful as follows:

Tourist Information	Fax	Phone
Bus Information	(01) 830 9377	(01) 836 6111
Train Information	(01) 874 5603	(01) 836 6222
IYHA (An Oige)	(01) 830 5808	(01) 830 4555
IHH (Independent Holiday Hostels)	(01) 836 4710	(01) 836 4700

Embassies		
Britain	(01) 205 3870	(01) 205 3700
Belgium	(01) 283 8488	(01) 269 2082
Denmark	(01) 478 4536	(01) 475 6404
France	(01) 283 0178	(01) 260 1666
Germany	(01) 269 3946	(01) 269 3011
Italy	(01) 668 2759	(01) 660 1744
Japan	(01) 283 8726	(01) 269 4244
Netherlands	(01) 283 9690	(01) 269 3444
Spain	(01) 269 1854	(01) 269 1640
USA	(01) 660 8469	(01) 668 8777

CORK

Bus	(021) 508188
Flight Information — Cork Airport	(021) 313131
Tourist Information	(021) 273251
Train Information	(021) 506766

Consulates

Belgium	(021) 277399
Denmark	(021) 276841
France	(021) 311800
Italy	(021) 275352
Netherlands	(021) 317900

GALWAY

Tourist Information	(091) 563081
Bus Information	(091) 562000
Train Information	(091) 561444
Island Ferries	(091) 568903
evenings	(091) 572273

GENERAL

Flight Information — Shannon Airport	(061) 471666
— Knock Airport (Horan International)	(094) 67222

SELECTED TOURIST INFORMATION OFFICES (OUTSIDE DUBLIN)

Waterford	(051) 75788
Wexford	(053) 23111
Killarney	(064) 31633
Ennis	(065) 28366
Cliffs of Moher	(065) 81171
Tralee	(066) 21288
Galway	(091) 563081
Westport	(098) 25711
Horan International Airport, Knock	(094) 67247
Sligo	(071) 61201
Letterkenny	(074) 21160
Dundalk	(042) 35484
Belfast	(01232) 327888
Derry	(01504) 369501
London	(0171) 493 3201
Paris	(1) 4261 8426
Frankfurt	(069) 236492
Amsterdam	(020) 223101
New York	(212) 418 0800
Toronto	(416) 364 1301

SELECTED TELEPHONE NUMBERS — NORTHERN IRELAND

The prefixes given for Northern Ireland are for use inside Northern Ireland and for dialling from the UK. If phoning from the Republic, note that you should first dial 08 then the particular prefix and number given.

Tourist Information Offices

59 North Street, Belfast	(01232) 246609
City Hall, Belfast	(01232) 320202 Ext. 2737
Belfast International Airport	(01849) 422888 Ext. 3009

Ballycastle, Co. Antrim	(012657) 62024
Giant's Causeway	(012657) 31855
Larne, Narrow Gauge Road	(01574) 260088
Newcastle, Co. Down	(013967) 22222
Warrenpoint, Co. Down	(016937) 52256
Enniskillen, Co. Fermanagh	(01365) 323110/325050
Coleraine, Co. Londonderry	(01265) 52181 (Council Office)
Derry City	(01504) 267284

Youth Hostels Association of Northern Ireland (YHANI)	(01232) 324733

Northern Ireland Railways Information

Belfast Central Station	(01232) 899411
Wellington Place, Belfast	(01232) 899400
Larne Harbour	(01574) 279221
Derry City	(01504) 42228

Other Useful Numbers

Ulsterbus	(01232) 333000
Sealink Belfast (office hours)	(01232) 747747
P & O Larne	(01574) 274400
Belfast International Airport	(01849) 422888
Belfast City Airport	(01232) 457745

Consulates

Belgium	(01846) 682671
Denmark	(01232) 230581
Finland	(016937) 72761
Germany	(01574) 260777
Greece	(01232) 242242
Italy	(01232) 668854
Netherlands (after 6 pm)	(01574) 261000
Norway	(01232) 242242
Portugal	(01232) 242242
Sweden	(01232) 230581
Turkey (office in London only)	(0044) 171 589 0949/589 0350
USA	(01232) 328239